A LIKELY TALE, LAD

A LIKELY TALE, LAD

Laughs & larks growing up in the 1970s

MIKE PANNETT

Dalesman

First published in 2014 by
Country Publications Ltd
The Water Mill, Broughton Hall
Skipton, North Yorkshire BD23 3AG
www.dalesman.co.uk

Paperback edition published in 2015

ISBN 978-1-85568-344-0

Text and cover design, typesetting, illustration
and titling typeface, 'Clumsy Baskerville'
by Lyn Davies Design.

Printed in China for Latitude Press Ltd.

CONTENTS

PLATES

AUTHOR'S NOTE

This is a story about my childhood. It's not quite the story of my childhood. I've allowed myself to take one or two liberties with dates and timing and even one or two locations, missing out a few dull bits, cramming all the good stuff into a few special years either side of our move into the countryside. But I've tried to be paint a faithful portrait of my family, and my close friends. Should an eagle-eyed reader spot an error or two in the chronology, or the geography, I'd say, 'Just take a look at the title of this book.' Because the clue's right there: this is a likely tale, lad.

To my late dad Jeff
(he would be proud) and my mother Shirley,
for putting up with me for all these years.
My brother Phil, and my sisters Christine (a big help
in remembering things) and Gillian.
I love them all.

Beside the Sea

'Right, inside with you.'

Mum had packed the sandwiches into the back, followed by the brown paper packages. One, two, three, four. They were, we well knew, our Easter eggs.

Dad, of course, had his head under the bonnet. He'd already conducted a final inspection of the car the previous day: water, oil, light bulbs, tyre pressures, checked with his special pressure gauge, and my big brother Phil and I had been given the task of washing it.

Now we were ready to depart.

I was standing on the drive with one foot inside the Morris Traveller, registration number TDN 6. I had my green Thunderbird 2 in my left hand, a bag of marbles in my right, and Petra's leash between my teeth. I was scanning the mound of luggage that was strapped to the roof-rack: three or four suitcases, several cardboard boxes, a wicker hamper and ... ah! There it was, protruding from one end of the tightly rolled, striped canvas windbreak: my fishing rod.

Satisfied that my most precious possession was safely on board, I lowered my head and looked into the car. Phil was hunched up by the far window, eyes closed, his transistor radio glued to his ear. My big sister Christine had bagged the near-side seat, with her Tiny Tears doll on her knee, her head buried in a copy of Jackie. The space in between – the space I was supposed to squeeze into – was occupied by my baby sister, Gillian, more or less buried under her huge rag doll, Jemima.

Behind the three of them, the rear windows were obscured by a jumble of boxes, blankets, towels, buckets, spades and a plastic football.

Mum gave the rear doors a final shove to get them to close.

'Come on, Michael, get a move on. Your Dad's almost ready.'

'There's no room, Mum,' I muttered, my tongue rasping against the braided leather leash. It had a nasty salty taste. I threw up my hands in a gesture of exasperation, at which Thunderbird 4 fell out of the back ramp of Thunderbird 2. 'Oh Mum, now look what you've done.'

'Never mind, Michael, you can pick it up.' Mum bent down and peered inside the car. 'Girls, squeeze up. Both of you.' They each leaned to one side, grudgingly, opening up a gap about nine inches wide. 'That's better. There you are, Michael – in the back with you.'

'Mum! Mu-um!' Gillian wailed as I swept her dolls into the foot-well, then turned and plonked myself down, half on her lap, half off it. 'He's sitting on my leg. He's squa-ashing me! And Jemima.'

Mum sighed. 'Well, do as I say and move over. Then he won't have to, will he?'

I squirmed my way into the narrow space between the two girls, digging my elbow into Christine's ribs. Petra jumped onto her lap. My big sister wrinkled up her nose and shoved the dog across onto me. 'She needs a bath.' She rubbed her hands on my shirt. 'And she's all … yuk. All greasy.'

'That's natural, that grease,' I said. I put my arms around the dog. 'All dogs have it. I saw it on Blue Peter. It makes 'em waterproof. Doesn't it, Petra?'

I wriggled some more, trying to get comfortable. I didn't mention that I'd been so worried about Petra's natural oils getting washed off when I took her down to the beck that I'd nicked some of Phil's Bryl-creem and rubbed it into her coat.

'Ow!' Now Christine was kicking off. 'Mum, Mum, can't you do something! He's pinching me.'

'Well, move over – like Mum said!' I shouted, giving her a shove. Christine had her arm raised and was all set to smack me in the face.

'Now, what did I tell you about fighting?' Mum eased herself into her seat and closed the door, addressing us via the rear-view mirror. 'I don't want another peep out of either of you or – or there'll be no fish and chips tonight. You hear me?'

Silence, just the sound of Dad closing the bonnet and putting away his oil can before locking the garage door.

'Well, are you going to answer me?'

'But you said you didn't want another peep ...' I began.

Dad was in the driving seat, wiping his hands on an old wash-leather. 'This is not the time for cleverness, Michael. You know very well what your mother means. Now, why don't we all take a deep breath and put a smile on our faces, eh?'

With that he pulled out the choke and fired up the engine, put his arm around the back of the passenger seat and started to reverse through the gate. 'Starboard look-out?' he said. My big brother opened his eyes, blinked and looked along the street. 'Yeah. Fine, Dad. Nobody about.'

Dad backed us out onto Park Avenue, put her in first gear and set off towards the end of the road. I leaned across the girls and peered through the open window to watch, fascinated, as the orange plastic indicator flipped up in readiness for the left turn onto the main road. At last. We were off. On our holidays.

Throughout my childhood, holidays meant one thing and one thing only: the long drive over the North York Moors to the coast at Staintondale. When I say it was a long drive you have to understand that Dad rarely did things the easy way. You only had to mention the A64, the main route which connects the east coast with Malton, York and the West Riding, and he'd shake his head.

'Dreadful road,' he'd say. 'Absolute death-trap. And traffic? D'you know, I once set off from York on a Sunday morning and there was a queue two miles long. They were backed up all the way from Malton to Huttons Ambo. No, I think we'll go the scenic way.'

And so we did. Instead of nipping up the A64 main road, then over to Pickering and across the moors, we took the back-roads. What would be a brisk fifty-mile run to the coast for any normal family became an epic, a feat of endurance, the stuff of Pannett legends. A journey that would take me one hour today took us anything up to five. It was meticulously planned, of course. The night before our departure, Dad would sit at the living room table, a freshly sharpened pencil in one hand, a notebook in the other, studying his dog-eared Ordnance Survey maps – the old ones, I mean, the kind that were printed on canvas. Mile by mile he'd go over the route we'd used last year, and the year before that, even taking out his ruler and protractor to measure round the bends to see whether he could find a quieter way to the coast, and maybe shave a few hundred yards or so off the distance to be covered, thereby reducing his outlay on petrol.

The results of his research meant that we always ended up bouncing down some dusty farm track or winding our way along near-deserted lanes that snaked between fields of wheat and barley. From time to time we'd have the excitement of a cattle-grid, and if we were behaving ourselves Dad would rattle across at speed and make us all giggle – even though he said it was bad for the suspension. Good for morale, but bad for the springs.

Every so often, we'd meet an oncoming vehicle and Dad, being a courteous knight of the road, would put the brakes on, sling the old Morris into reverse and back up two, three, four hundred yards to let some flat-hatted farmer go past in a mud-spattered Land Rover, showering us with dust and chippings, acknowledging our good manners with a barely perceptible nod of the head or a stubby index finger raised languidly from the steering-wheel. And as he backed up, Mum would nod and smile.

'Well done, Jeff dear. Did you see, children, how well your father reversed the car there?'

We made our way across country to Sheriff Hutton, and there we faced our first challenge. Terrington Bank. Could we get up it in one run without having to bail out? 'You need a good run, a bit of momentum,' Dad said as he put his foot down, gripped the wheel and gritted his teeth.

By now, barely a quarter of the way to our destination, somebody would be pleading for a toilet break, and everybody else would agree that that was a good idea because they were bursting too. But it would have to wait until we'd tackled a much stiffer climb on the approach to Nunnington – and listened for the umpteenth time to Mum and Dad's running commentary about the war and the munitions dump that used to be hidden in the woods just a couple of miles from where we were, on the outskirts of Hovingham.

'Right, time to lighten the load, everybody. Chance to stretch those legs, get some fresh air in your lungs.'

And as he brought the car to a halt, out we got, all of us – even Mum – and walked up the incline, while he drove to the top. There he lifted the bonnet to help the engine cool, lit a cigarette, and strolled out to admire the scenery until we re-joined him, puffing and panting.

As soon as we'd caught up with him it was back inside for the short run down to Nunnington, our first designated stop. Here we'd all pile out and hurry across the pasture to where the trees lined the riverbank. Boys to one side, girls to the other, after which we all realised we were hungry, and thirsty, and started badgering Mum for a snack – those of us who weren't down at the water's edge, that is.

'Michael, who told you to get your fishing rod out? You'll have plenty of time for that when we get to Staintondale, d'you hear?'

'But, Mum... this is the River Rye. There's eight-pound trout in here.'

'Says who?' Philip was standing there, grinning at me. 'Go on, who told you that?'

'Grandpa. Grandpa told me there was.'

'Were,' said Dad. 'Grandpa told you that there were.'

'Never mind his grammar,' Mum said. 'Tell him to stow that rod before he puts our Gillian's eye out.'

After a drink of Tizer and a banana sandwich, after we'd persuaded Petra to come out of the river and all had a good shriek as she shook herself dry and soaked our legs in the process, we piled back in the old Traveller, opened the windows to get rid of the smell of wet dog, and made our way across towards the A170, past the remains of Wombleton Airfield, where Mum would tell us, yet again, about the old airbase.

'Those bombs they hid in Hovingham woods, this is where they brought them. For the Halifax bombers.' Then she'd go quiet. 'Very brave young men,' she'd say, and Dad would nod his head before patting the steering wheel. 'Running nice and smoothly,' he'd say, 'if that's not tempting fate.'

I don't know how long Dad had had the Morris Traveller. It seemed as though it had always been with us. It never occurred to me that there might have been a time when he wasn't taking the engine to bits in the garage on a weekend, and somehow managing to put it back together in time for our three-times-a-year trip to Staintondale, or the occasional run into town to watch York City play. That pale green car with its lovingly varnished woodwork, its creaky leather seats, its orange plastic trafficators and picture-book headlights, seemed like a part of the furniture, a revered and respected elder of the family. I couldn't remember a time when it wasn't there, like a faithful old servant, waiting to take us away. But, like any servant, it needed looking after, and Dad was determined it would 'see us out', as he put it. I used to worry that he meant it had to last us till we died, which I guessed would be in about a hundred years' time at the very least, but I eventually realised what he meant: that it had to keep going until we were old enough to provide for our own transport, by which time he might be able to afford a replacement. The point is, he nursed that car, and that's why we had to get out and walk the steep hills.

We didn't complain. Perhaps we were grateful that we hadn't come by way of Rosedale, as we did some years, and had to walk up the Chimney Bank with its 1-in-3 gradient. For that one we marched single file with as much luggage as we could carry and held our breath as the car lurched on in second gear, then first, before giving a thankful gasp as it finally made it to the top with us barely fifty yards behind it. But what a view when we got there – out towards the coast in one direction, the Pennines the other way, and the outline of Birdsall Brow with its top-knot of trees, fifteen or twenty miles to the south.

We drove on, towards the next major landmark. The A170 runs to the coast from Thirsk. It always loomed large in my mind as a vital staging-post, long before I knew anything about road numbers, well before I had any sense of the geography of North Yorkshire. That road always had a sort of mythic status for me, thanks to the way Dad spoke of it.

'Once we make it to the A170,' he would say, as if we were traversing the Sahara en route to the equator, 'once we've got that behind us we can all relax. Cross the A170 and we can all get in a proper holiday mood.'

He was thinking of our picnic lunch on the moors, when we'd pull off the road onto a stretch of close-cropped grass and devour a great pile of meat-paste sandwiches while he took out his Primus stove and brewed up the tea. After that he and Mum would doze on a blanket for half an hour while we kids – and the dog, of course – explored the patch of country around us and paddled in one of the moorland streams. Sometimes we'd play cowboys and Indians, sometimes cops and robbers. That was Petra's favourite. At home we'd already trained her to chase cars and bikes down the road, and now I'd taught her to play dead. 'Bang! Bang!' I'd shout and down she'd go, flat to the ground, head on her paws as she waited for the signal to get up.

Back in the driver's seat, Dad checked the fuel gauge and made a note in his little book. He kept meticulous records of distances covered and fuel consumed. 'Burns a lot of petrol, a hill like that,' he said. And we knew that as soon as he came to a decent downhill stretch he'd cut the engine, slip the clutch and let it roll, grinning as he did so. 'Of course, strictly speaking it's against the law,' he'd say, 'but this'll pay us back for all that climbing.' He was very Yorkshire, our Dad. Waste not, want not.

'Look at that, thirty-five miles an hour – forty! – and it's not costing us a penny.' Dad was all but crowing. Mum gripped the edge of her seat, closed her eyes and said nothing.

Once we were properly out in the country it seemed that half the roads we drove along were bordered with wide verges. Some even had a lush green strip growing down the middle where the surface had cracked. So when we came across the inevitable flock of sheep there was nothing for it but to wait patiently while they nibbled the grass and the ubiquitous black-and-white border collie tried to round them up, snapping at our tyres if we dared get within fifty yards of his charges. Meanwhile, of course, Petra was snarling and scrabbling at the windows, darting from one side of the car to the other, even diving into the front seat to hurl herself at the windscreen.

'Dad, Dad,' I pleaded, 'can't we let Petra out? Ple-ease say we can.'

I had visions of the flock parting like the Red Sea, the sheepdog scuttling home with its tail between its legs, and Petra leading us triumphantly onwards, to the coast, with her reward between her jaws – a big juicy marrow-bone.

'Ple-ease, Dad. You always said a dog should earn its keep …'

Dad laughed and shoved the manic Petra over his shoulder and into the back seat. 'I did, didn't I? And I'm sure she'll fetch us a rabbit or two once we get to the farm. Hello – looks like they're going into that field there.' And with that he fired the car up once more and on we went, at a nice steady twenty-five miles an hour as Dad calculated how many more miles it was to the farm and when we might arrive.

'There they are.' Dad would be pointing towards the horizon and the three enormous white 'golf balls', the early-warning system at RAF Fylingdales. 'They do a fine job, those things. Keep this country safe, let me tell you.'

'How does it work, Dad?'

'It's all very secret, Michael. I'll maybe tell you when you're a bit older.' And he'd put a finger to his mouth. 'Loose lips sink ships, and all that.'

It all sounded very James Bond. I had visions of Sean Connery strolling around inside in a black sweater, gun at the ready – or maybe fighting some evil foreigner on the top of the golf balls. We all knew that Dad was doing some sort of engineering work for the forces, but he wasn't allowed to tell us what it was exactly, and that made it all the more intriguing.

'Here we go! Mungo Jerry.' Phil had hardly said a word the entire trip, but now he pulled his earphones out of the radio, turned it up full blast, and we all sang along. 'In the summer time, when the weather is fine. In the summer time ... I got women I got women on my mind.'

'All except you.' He nudged me in the ribs. 'All you've got on your mind is your blinking fishing rod, you little weed.' And with that he plugged himself back in and closed his eyes again.

It was mid-afternoon when we made the final approach to Stain-tondale, along a single-track road which crossed a moss-covered stone bridge before rising sharply towards the farm house. 'Oh no!' Christian and Gillian led a chorus of complaints as we were turfed out for one more march uphill.

But it wasn't far now, and we were soon driving into the farmyard, scattering the hens, the geese and two stray piglets. The sheepdogs, chained up around the yard, mostly ignored us, just lay there with their heads on their paws, taking it all in. I don't think they liked having us invade the place – particularly as they had to tolerate Petra, who strolled around the yard with a superior air, off her lead, while they remained securely tethered until they were summoned for work.

I don't know how the connection was first made, but for generations our family had taken holidays at White House Farm. It was occupied by three sisters, Annie, Maud and Doris. To us they were all Aunties, and here they were to greet us as we piled out of the car. Mum and Dad were stiff and yawning after the journey, but as they greeted their friends we kids shouted a brief 'Hello!' and scampered across the yard to see who could get to the milking barn first – all except Phil, who was still glued to his radio in the back seat of the car.

In the barn we found Billy and Jack, the two brothers who worked on the farm, and always had done as far as we knew. The pair of them seemed as old as the hills to me, with their brown leather boots with the long row of shiny buttons, their corduroy trousers tied by a length of string below the knee, Billy's shapeless flat hat and Jack's white clay pipe. That pipe was always smouldering. Some days, when he was having one of his forgetful turns, you'd see a wisp of smoke coming out of his jacket pocket as he wandered around the yard scratching his head and asking you if you'd seen it.

'Now then, young feller-me-lad. Aren't they feeding you back at your place?'

'What do you mean?' Billy was always talking in riddles, it seemed to me.

Jack laughed and sat on a straw bale. 'Why, he means you don't seem to have grown much since your last visit. Reckon you could do with some of Doris's home cooking. Fatten you up for market.' He patted his own ample belly and added, 'Look at us – like a couple of little porkers, aren't we? And it's all her doing, bless her.'

I stood up straight, puffed out my chest and flexed my biceps. 'I'm almost four foot six,' I said. 'And guess what?'

'Ooh, I'm no good at guessing,' Jack said. 'You'll have to tell me, lad.'

'I'm the fastest runner in our class. I won the hundred yards dash on sports day.'

'In that case I reckon you're big enough and strong enough to lend us a hand wi' milking them cows when they come in. You'd like that, wouldn't you, lad?' He knew I would. It was one of my favourite jobs around the place. 'Well then,' Billy said, 'why don't you go and see if the ladies have got a spot of afternoon tea laid out for you. By the time you're done there them cows should be ready.'

The girls had gone to look at an orphan calf. Billy and Jack were keeping it in a pen with a mother who'd lost her own youngster in the hope that she'd adopt it. Any time now the rest of the herd, all black-and-white Friesians, would come ambling across the pasture and gather at the five-barred gate for evening milking. The farm had a proper modern set-up in the big shed, with electrically operated vacuum pumps, but they still milked the one Jersey cow, Amanda, the old-fashioned way, and made their own dairy products in a little room off the farmhouse kitchen. Often we would be allowed to ride Amanda in from the field for milking – with Billy and Jack walking either side. Amanda was what they called the house cow. Her milk was creamier than the Friesians, perfect for butter and cheese.

Back in the house I got the usual hugs – one from each of the sisters in turn. Although they were sisters, and looked very much alike – like peas from the same pod, as Mum always said – you could tell them apart with your eyes shut. Annie always smelled of lavender, while Maud wore eau de cologne. I was getting to that age when I tried my best to avoid hugs – especially from plump old ladies like them – but the one person I never minded wrapping her arms around me was Doris. Doris always gave off an enticing aroma – of things like cinnamon, or almond essence, or vanilla. She was the baker in the family, and it was one of her wonderful creations that I spotted on the cooling-rack as she sat Mum and Dad down at the scrubbed pine table and filled the teapot from the big black kettle that seemed to simmer on the old stove all day long, whatever the weather.

'Why don't you children carry your Mum and Dad's cases upstairs while I cut this cake and let the tea brew,' Doris said. 'Go on – won't take you a couple of minutes; give us chance for a bit of grown-up talk. And here, fill that bowl under the sink there; give your dog a drink. Look at the poor old lass, she's panting like a traction engine.'

Phil had come in from the car at last, and he gave the dog her water while Gillian, Christine and I lugged the cases up the narrow staircase and along the landing where the dark, bare floorboards always seemed to creak no matter how carefully you trod. Even in the middle of the night when you were lying in bed you'd sometimes hear them. Dad said it was just settlement as the house cooled down, but I was convinced it was ghosts. Normally that would've terrified me, but we all slept in the same room – one bed for the girls, another for me and Phil – so I felt safe enough. They were old-fashioned sprung beds with thick feather quilts and big downy pillows. There was even a china pot under each one, not that we ever used those. Dad said they were for the winter nights.

'When I used to stay here, back in the days when we had proper winters,' he liked to say, 'and before they had the inside privy built, believe me, a fellow could freeze to death going out in that yard. Those days we had to heat a brick up by the fire and wrap it in an old blanket to act as a hot water bottle. Otherwise our toes would've dropped off. Imagine.'

Back downstairs, after we'd demolished Doris's fruit cake, she got me to wind the grandfather clock that stood at one end of the kitchen. When I say kitchen you have to understand that theirs was a huge room – at least, it seemed so to me. The sink and the cooker were at one end, next to the Aga. The other end was where we all ate, around the table. There was a pine dresser too, with all the aunties' best china on display; there was a single rocking chair with a hand-made rug under it, and beside that was the grandfather clock. At night it was so quiet, the ticking of the clock was all you could hear. If you opened it up you could still read the maker's name, and the date. 1786. The story went that it had been made by a young clock-maker who'd come to the end of his apprenticeship and had to produce a finished item to prove that he'd learned his trade properly. It was what they called his masterpiece. I'd always been fascinated with the clock. Even when I was barely able to stand I used to watch as one of the sisters took the big metal key and opened the glazed front. Then she'd open the tall wooden door as well, exposing the pulleys and what they called the 'mice', the heavy cast-iron weights that rose to the top in a series of jerks as she wound it up. They used to let Phil do it, then Christine, and now it was a job I was deemed able to take on – under close supervision.

Back in the milking parlour, the cows were all standing in their stalls, the machinery humming. I loved it in there. You could hear the milk sloshing around in pipes and emptying into the stainless steel vessels. Occasionally a cow would stamp a foot, or snort, or drop a huge wet turd on the straw-covered floor, which always made me laugh. Billy was checking that the animals were all comfortable. 'Here,' he said, pointing to the far corner where the solitary Amanda stood next to the stool I'd fetched out earlier, 'you know what to do, don't you?'

Of course I did. It was only a few months since Billy had finally given in to my pestering and taught me. I positioned the three-legged stool carefully. I didn't want a repeat of my first attempt, when the cow stepped back and trod on me. You've no idea how heavy they are until you feel the full weight of one on your foot. And I didn't want her kicking me, as happened to Phil one time. He carried that bruise for weeks afterwards, and it turned just about every colour of the rainbow.

On this occasion, though, Billy had placed a tub of food at the head end of the cow. 'Just regular old cattle nuts,' he said. Then he winked at me. 'Sweetened 'em wi' a bit of molasses. That's the secret, lad. They can't resist it. Keeps her occupied while you pull on the old teats, d'you see?'

I was soon sat there, squirting the warm milk into the shiny galvanised bucket that I gripped between my knees, occasionally leaning forward to aim it into my mouth and savour the sweetness. There really is nothing quite like it. I was enjoying every moment of the task until my big brother crept up behind me, grabbed a teat and showered the milk all over my shorts.

'I'll get you for that!' I shouted. But he was already gone, pausing at the door to shout, 'No you won't. Too slow to catch a cold, you are. See you at the beach!' And he was off, his fishing rod in his hand.

I'm afraid poor Amanda got short shrift after that. Phil had reminded me that the whole point of coming to Staintondale was to get down to the sea. I tugged away manically, barely bothering to take aim, and was soon standing in a puddle of milk, my feet squelching inside my shoes. The cow had abandoned her bowl of goodies and was stamping her irritation. I decided I had enough in my pail, hurried back across the yard and handed it to Maud. She was responsible for producing the cream, buttermilk, butter and an occasional slab of cheese for the household. 'Hm, not a lot today,' she said, peering into the half-filled pail. She went to the window and looked out at the sky. 'Maybe it's them clouds,' she said. 'They do tend to go off it when the weather turns.'

'Yes,' I said, trying to sound as though I knew what I was talking about. 'The weather. That's what Billy reckoned too.' Then I rushed out to the car, pulled out my fishing rod, my bag of hooks, spare line and other bits and pieces, checked that I had my knife in my pocket, and set off.

'Where you going now, lad?' Jack was just coming out of the big barn, pausing to strike a match on the wall and put it to his clay pipe.

'To the beach,' I said.

'You mean the wyke, lad.' He was referring to its proper name, Hayburn Wyke. Dad had told us all about that. He'd read it in a book he got out of the library. According to him, 'wyke' came from a Viking word. It meant a cove or an inlet, some little spot where you might land a long-boat in amongst the cliffs, hidden from view. 'And what d'you reckon to catch down there, lad? Couple of codling, maybe?'

'Aye. We got one last year. Two and a half pounds it weighed.'

'Ah,' Jack said. 'Codling's not bad – although you'll have more chance of catching them towards the back end of t'year.' Then he took his pipe from his mouth, tamped the tobacco down with his forefinger, and said, 'What you want to be going after is trout. In the beck down yonder. Has nobody ever taken the trouble to teach you how to tickle a trout?'

I didn't answer at first. I was still looking at his hand, wondering how he could bear to put his finger into the bowl of his pipe like that, what with the tobacco glowing red and smoking. I'd seen him do it any number of times and I still couldn't work out how he managed it. 'No,' I said, 'they haven't.'

'Well, you take yourself off now – and in a day or two you come and have a word with me. Maybe on the weekend when things is a bit quieter. Then we'll see if we can't mek a proper fisherman of you. How's that, eh?'

'Wow, that'd be fantastic,' I said, before hurrying on, across the little paddock and into the wood, puzzling all the way as to what he might mean by tickling them.

To get down to the wyke you had to duck under a lot of low-growing branches and watch out for badger-holes, fallen limbs, trailing creepers. You had to cross three separate streams and be careful not to skid on the wet stones. And then came the best part, slithering down beside the waterfall that tumbled down the cliff into a deep pool surrounded by rocks, just above the high tide line. Then you were out on the sand, in a bay, more or less deserted apart from the occasional hiker doing the Cleveland Way – and the odd angler who knew what a great spot it was.

When I got there Phil was already out on our rock, ducking to avoid the spray as a wave crashed lazily against it, turning to grin at me as he tugged on his line. 'Got one!' he shouted. 'Got one!' He was reeling it in as fast as he could, and there, on the end of his line, was a wriggling, glistening young cod. 'Must be a two-pounder, at least,' he called out.

What we called our rock was a huge boulder, a great slab, thirty or forty yards from the base of the cliff. Even at low tide it was tricky to get to it because of the slippery rocks surrounding it. You had to keep your eye on the tide to avoid getting wet on the way back. Once you'd scrambled up on to it, it was reasonably level. You could set out your things, bait your line and cast into quite deep water.

Phil had landed the fish. He whacked its head on the rock, and slid the hook out. Then he snapped his fingers at me. 'Knife. Where is it?'

'Where's yours?'

He jerked a thumb back towards the cliff. 'Must've slipped out of my pocket when we were in the car. C'mon, hand it over.'

'Why should I? After you squirted all that milk down me.'

'That was just a joke. Now come on, gimme the knife. Or do you want me to come and get it off you?'

My Swiss Army knife was one of my prized possessions. It had caused quite a stir at home as Mum wasn't sure I was old enough for it. But my Dad had backed me up. For a boy who liked playing in the woods, making bow and arrows – and of course fishing – it was absolutely essential. For survival. I pulled it slowly out of my pocket. 'Only if we share the fish,' I said.

Phil stood there for a moment, scowling. Then his face broke into a grin. 'Aye, all right then. Fair enough.' And with that he dropped the fish at my foot. 'But you've got to clean it.' He gathered his things together. 'See you back at the farm, sucker.'

You never really got the better of Phil. Who does get the better of a big brother? Still, as far as I was aware I'd got an honourable draw. The only trouble was, when I finally got back, wet through, my fingers stinging where I'd nicked them with the knife, and with the two halves of the codling stuffed into my trousers – one in each pocket – the whole family were standing by the car waiting for me. Dad was tapping his wristwatch. 'Come on, Michael,' he said. 'Have you forgotten? It's fish and chips tonight. Now get in that car, and be quick about it.'

I dived into my seat. The girls shrank from my wet shirt, and shrieked dutifully when I pulled the dead fish out and waved it in their faces. 'Just wait till tomorrow,' I said, 'after me and Billy have gone tickling trout. Then I'll really make you jump.'

'Downhill all the way!' Dad was all but purring – and so was the old Traveller as we freewheeled towards Scarborough. We were all in high spirits. Eating fried haddock and chips out of a newspaper while we wandered around the harbour watching the bobbing fishing boats was a real treat. The rest of the week, our meals would be home cooked by Doris, followed by quiet evenings playing board games and cards, or just chatting by the fire – if it was deemed cool enough to light one. There was no television out there, and Mum and Dad seemed to like that. It gave the family time together without the distractions of work, homework and all the other madness of our home life. And, as Dad liked to remind us, if war broke out there was plenty of grub and we could listen to the old valve radio in the sisters' living room. Just now, though, peace reigned, and we could sit by the open fire with the toasting forks Mum had packed and make a bedtime snack of hot buttered crumpets.

Tickling Trout

'Now then.'

Whenever Jack uttered those two words, I knew I had to take note. That's the great thing about being the age I was then: you listen to what the old folk tell you, and you take it in. Later on, as you start to grow up, you get this foolish idea that they're too old and you're too clever – and you stop listening. You shrug off their advice. What do they know? By the time it finally strikes you that some of them actually talked a lot of sense, that some of them knew just about everything worth knowing, why, they're most likely dead and buried. It's just as Jack said to me one day when we were standing by a moss-covered gravestone in Cloughton cemetery. We'd gone to look at his ancestors' resting-place, and I remember watching, mouth agape, as he tapped out his pipe against the back of the headstone and said, 'There's more wisdom buried under these slabs than you'll find in any book, lad.' He sighed and added, 'It's been the same old story – since the dawn of time.' With that, he looked at me, tapped his pipe once more, patted the headstone, and grinned at me. 'Don't worry, lad. My old granddad enjoyed the smell of a good tobacco.'

Looking back, I can see how lucky I was in those days. Jack and Billy were a couple of wise old birds. I used to wish that we had teachers like them at school. I learned such a lot from them. I must have been about eight years old when Jack took me aside that morning and told me to follow him. He never said what was on his mind, but of course I didn't ask. All would be revealed.

'Now then,' he said, as we headed across the dusty yard, scattering the hens and arousing the interest of the cockerel – a beast of a thing that would attack your legs on the slightest provocation, 'first job we need to do is sharpen our knives. We can't go fishing with blunt in-struments, can we now?'

'No,' I said. I was all ears. It was the first I'd heard that we were go-ing fishing. I hurried along beside him and followed him in through the doorway that led to the workshop he and Billy used, right beside the big barn. There, under the dim light of a single electric bulb, he took out a dark grey rectangular stone, a whetstone he called it, and placed it on a blackened work-bench, next to a big iron vice.

'Now,' he said, sweeping a pile of wood shavings onto the floor, 'fetch us down a can of oil, will you?'

I gazed around at the clutter of hammers and drills, the coils of rope and wire, the mysterious tools with worn wooden handles and strangely shaped metal parts, the old Oxo tin full of nuts and bolts, the tobacco tins and jam-jars full of miscellaneous hardware, the many and varied saws hanging from butcher's hooks. I was looking for a gallon container of Castrol, such as Dad had in his garage for the Traveller.

'Up yonder,' he said, pointing to a shelf right above my head. 'The bicycle oil, d'you see her?'

I passed him the can of Three-in-One and watched, fascinated, as he poured an S-shaped squiggle of it onto the stone, then took from his pocket a knife, its blade perhaps four inches long, and curved. I don't mean curved like mine was, a gentle convex sort of curve; no, his was curved inwards as if it had been eaten away, which I suppose it had. It had been rendered concave by a thousand sharpenings over goodness knows how many years. It was thin and pointed, like a bon-ing knife. A bit frightening, really.

'Had this little beauty since I wasn't much taller than what you are,' he said, and started to work the blade to and fro in the puddle of oil, pausing every so often to check its edge with his thumb. 'Touch and go whether it wears out before I do. And see that handle? My old Dad made that out of a piece of juniper. Lovely and smooth, and do you know, it kept its scent for years. All gone now, of course,' he said, and he held the handle out for me to sniff. It smelled of oil, and tobacco.

'Now you have a go,' he said.

I took out my Swiss Army knife and opened up the big blade. Placing it on the carborundum stone, I did my best to imitate Jack's movements. He didn't comment, just corrected me once or twice with a touch of his hand to get the angle right, and smiled approvingly when it seemed I'd got the hang of it, with the blade pressed almost level with the stone and the blackened oil forming a sort of ripple around it. He waited until I'd done both sides, took it off me and tested it with his thumb, nodded, and turned the whetstone over.

'This here,' he said, 'this is your smooth side – rubs off any jagged bits and gets a proper edge on it. Stops it catching too. I always say a blunt knife's more dangerous than a properly sharpened one. Get a proper edge and it'll cut nice and smooth, with no snagging. You don't want it snagging, lad. That's how you're liable to nick your fingers.'

I agreed that I didn't want that, and started to work the blade once more.

By the time we'd finished Jack reckoned I'd be able to shave my chin with my knife – if I had any whiskers to shave, that was.

'Now,' he said, replacing the oil-can and the whetstone on their shelf, 'that's all you need to go tickling trout – that and a plastic bag. Mind,' he added, 'in my day we never had no plastic bags. You shoved your catch down your shirt front or into your trouser pocket. Then you ran like the wind.'

'Why was that?' I asked. 'Why did you have to run?'

Jack laughed and ruffled my hair. He looked around him as if he thought somebody might be listening. 'Because, lad, they weren't our fish to catch.'

I suppose I was still looking puzzled.

He lowered his voice almost to a whisper and leaned forward. 'The thing is, we were … we were poaching. D'you see? But you're not to tell anyone, you hear?' And he pressed his finger to his lips as he ushered me out into the yard and closed the door behind us. Before we set off he looked at my sandaled feet. He was wearing a pair of green wellies. 'Aye, you could've done wi' a pair of rubber boots too.'

Ever since Jack first mentioned it, the idea of catching my own supper had taken a grip on me. And now we were off to the woods to make it a reality. Me and him. I followed in silence as he led the way into the wood, down the narrow, leaf-filled path that snaked between the trees. After a few hundred yards he signalled me to stop and listen. There was no wind in there, and the only sound, apart from a pigeon cooing in the tree-tops, was of running water. 'Aye, nearly there,' he said.

Down beside the little beck he told me to take a deep breath. I did as he said. 'From here on we've to be quiet as mice,' he said. 'Don't want to be disturbing them little fishes, do we now? So, nice and quiet, eh?' He looked at me with his stubby forefinger pressed to his lips, then said, 'All right, lad, you can breathe out now.'

I watched Jack as he stood there, peering into the brown-tinted water which tumbled over the rocks and dispersed into quiet pools shaded by the alders and long grass that grew on either side of the main stream. 'Do you see owt?' he asked. I scanned the surface of the stream. The only movement that caught my eye was the dark, rotting leaves that were being turned over by the current. I shook my head. 'Why, I reckon there's one there,' he said, 'just where you're standing.'

Bending down I now glimpsed the shadowy outline of a fish. For a few seconds it was quite still. Then it darted away, briefly illuminated by the dappled sunlight before it slid into the darkness under the bank. I expected Jack to show me how to grab it, but instead he said,

'We'll tek note of where he is and see if we can spot another one, eh?' With that he took off his hat, placed it on the mossy cushion above the trout's hiding-place and gestured to me to move on.

We made our way slowly upstream, moving carefully to avoid treading on any sticks. Every so often there would be a 'plop' and Jack's hand would go up and we'd both stand quite still. He'd lean forward, crouching, gazing into the water. Then he'd shake his head and move forward again. I was getting anxious now. Surely we wouldn't be going home empty handed? The others would all laugh at me. Phil had caught his codling the other day and he'd not let me forget it.

'Sshh!' Jack was down on all fours. He slipped his right hand into the water, closed his eyes and felt under the overhanging bank. Then he caught his breath, turned and winked at me. 'Now,' he said, 'you come and put your hand in, right here.' I edged towards him. 'Nice and slow, mind. No splashing. We don't want to startle him, do we?' It was colder than I'd expected, but the shiver that ran up my spine was nothing to do with the temperature. It was pure anticipation.

'Just have a feel around under there.' Jack said. 'No sudden movements. Nice and slow.' He stayed where he was and I extended my arm, reaching deep under the bank. Nothing. Then the river-bank itself, a slick wall of clay. 'Are you finding owt, lad?'

I shook my head once more. I could feel the current – slower here than in mid-stream and carrying little bits of debris through my fingers; I could feel one or two slippery roots, and now my fingers had reached the silky soft mud at the very bottom. But trout? No. I moved slowly forward, my hand still in the water as I crawled over the damp grass, wincing as my knee pressed onto a buried stone. All the time I watched Jack for a sign. He was standing there perfectly still, his head cocked to one side. I was starting to wonder whether there was anything there at all. He'd warned me from the outset that you needed patience. Infinite patience, he said, and that was something which, according to Mum, I didn't know the meaning of.

A loud splash interrupted my musings, and there was Jack, on his feet. In his hands was a dripping, wriggling trout. He held it out for me to see. It was a lovely thing: small, slender, shapely, its sides covered with the distinctive dark spots.

'Wow! You got it.'

'Aye, but he's only little, isn't he? Nowhere near fully grown. Let's put him back in, shall we? Go and see if that big 'un's still hiding. Maybe you can pull him out for me, eh?'

'I'll try,' I said, and watched as Jack dropped his catch into the water. I felt disappointed as it swam quickly across to the far bank. It might be the only one we caught.

We made our way back to where Jack had left his hat. I got down on all fours. He nodded approvingly as I dipped my hand in the water once more. Below me there was a pool. It was deep, deeper than I could reach without immersing my arm to the shoulder and undercutting the bank by a foot or so. I trembled as the water soaked my rolled-up shirt-sleeve. Was the big trout still there, or had it slipped away? No, it was there all right and my finger-tips were touching its under-belly. My heart was pounding. I held my breath and looked at Jack. It wouldn't bite me, would it?

'Found it?' he whispered.

'Aye.'

'Right then, just tickle him, real gently. Under his tummy, like I told you – and work your way forward, mind. Along the body towards his head.'

The fact was, I couldn't tell which end of the fish I was touching, but Jack had said how they always like to swim upstream so maybe … I worked my way forward, inch by inch along the cool, slippery body. Leaning forward as far as I dared without losing my balance, I peered into the water. 'I can see him!' I gasped. He was lying dead still, just his tail fin twitching ever so slightly.

'Right, lad. Now just tickle him under t'gills. You've to be ever so gentle, mind.' I did as Jack said. 'Then close your fingers round him – nice and firm.' That was the hard part. I was sure the fish would struggle, but I followed Jack's instructions to the letter. 'And have him out. Come on, lad. Before he wakes up.'

I was torn between conflicting impulses. On the one hand I was determined to hang on tight and not let my supper escape. On the other I felt a pity for the poor thing. I could now feel the tension as it began to arch its body, twisting one way and then the other. I gripped tight and stood up, my eyes fixed on its gaping mouth.

'Now, you can either whack its head on that rock,' Jack said, 'or get your finger in its mouth and pull its head back – but make your mind up, because the longer you leave it the more it'll suffer.'

Since those days I've learned to despatch a fish swiftly and efficiently. There's no need to prolong the agony. But on this occasion Jack had to help me out. 'Here,' he said, and took it from my hand before stepping into the water and killing it with a sharp blow on the nearest rock.

'Now,' he continued, holding out his hand, 'where's that knife of yours. I'll show you how we clean 'em – because this, my lad, is going in the pan for your supper tonight. Fresh caught trout and a big slice of bread and butter.' He smacked his lips and grinned. 'A meal fit for a king.'

I had my knife in my hand and was opening it with stiff, chilled fingers. 'How do I do it?' I asked. 'How do I clean it?' The truth was, I wasn't looking forward to seeing the fish's insides. I was thinking of the offal we sometimes put in a dish for the cat at home. Luckily, though, Jack didn't give me time to think about just how yukky its guts might be. He laid the now still fish on the rock and placed a gnarled forefinger on its side, just behind the gills. 'Right, lad, you put the point of your blade right there.' I did as he said. 'Then push in – go on, nice and firm.' I was surprised at how easily my newly sharpened blade penetrated the flesh. 'Aye, then you draw it down to the belly – that's right, and follow the belly down to the vent.'

'What's the vent?' I asked.

'Why, it's his bottom, lad. Where he does his business from. Come on now, don't be all day about it.'

I made the cut just as he said. 'Right, now you can slide your finger in and pull his guts out.' He could see me hesitate. 'Or use your blade. Go on, lad, it ain't as bad as you think.'

He was right. I was surprised at how little there was to the fish's insides. Just a couple of livery bits and a thin, pink tube. I scraped them out onto the rock and held the fish up for him to see. It was eight or nine inches long, and plump.

'Right, now it's my turn. You wander off downstream a little way and wash it, eh? While I catch one for meself.'

It didn't take Jack long, and the way he killed and cleaned it – well, it was like poetry. One stroke of the knife, a deft movement with his hand and there it was, one fat little trout, ready for the pan. He picked up his hat, plonked it on his head, shoved his catch in his trouser pocket and turned towards home. 'We'll maybe give these to Doris to fry for us, eh? Or would you rather do it in my shed there? I keep a little burner and a pan for when I fancy a fry-up on me own.'

I didn't answer him at first. In fact, we walked almost all the way back in silence. I was worried.

'Jack,' I said, just before we emerged into the field that adjoined the house.

'What is it, lad?'

'You know what you said about when you went catching trout? When you were little, I mean, and how you had to run like the wind.'

He didn't answer for a moment, just plodded on until he came to the stile. There he stopped so suddenly that I almost bumped into him.

'What is it?' he asked. 'What's bothering you, lad?'

I was frightened to ask him the question, but I wanted to know. 'Well, are we – I mean, is what we did poaching?'

Jack didn't answer at first. He sat on the wooden step, took out his pipe and lit it, puffed a couple of times and said, 'D'you know, I believe if anybody had seen us they might have said it was. But I don't think they did, do you?'

I could tell what he meant by the twinkle in his eye. 'No,' I said. 'And does that mean …?'

'Aye, I think it means we'd best fry these in t'workshop, don't you? Just in case anybody asks any awkward questions.'

Half an hour later, after he'd sent me to the house to scrounge some bread and butter and I'd told Doris that it was for Jack, that he was too busy to come in for his tea, I sat on a big fat log and watched as his little pot-belly stove started to roar and the butter spluttered in the frying pan.

'Of course,' he said, 'it weren't rightly poaching as such.'

'Oh, wasn't it?'

To tell the absolute truth I was a bit disappointed to hear that. I'd got used to the idea that we were poachers, and I was beginning to think that it was quite a glamorous thing to be. Seeing as I had plans to be a pirate one day, this seemed a necessary step along the road.

Jack lay the fish in the pan. Using the slender blade of his knife he started spreading butter on the fat crusts of home-baked bread.

'The way I see it,' he said, 'we were just having a little rest by the beck. I don't know about you, lad, but I stopped to wash, and blow me if that fish didn't jump right into me hands. What about you?'

'Aye,' I said, 'mine too.' I had a think for a moment, then added, 'He jumped out of the beck and – and bashed his head on a stone.'

'You've got the idea,' Jack said, and lifted the fish carefully, peering underneath. 'Aye, just crisping up nicely. How's your appetite, lad?'

Can I Drive a Bulldozer
When I Grow Up?

'Dad?'

He didn't answer immediately. He was concentrating on his driving. We'd left Staintondale later than planned and as a result Dad had decided to take the main road. Now, as we crept along in the heavy weekend traffic, he was regretting it.

'Yes, what is it, Michael?'

'Why can't we go and live in the country?'

Dad sighed. 'We've had this conversation before, haven't we? And I've explained why we can't.'

'Yeah but – '

I was stopped before I could utter a word of complaint. Dad braked sharply and muttered something about female drivers. Then he said, 'You can't just go and live wherever you want to. You've got to think about your livelihood.'

'Your father's talking about work,' Mum said.

'Well, couldn't you get a job on a farm, like Billy and Jack?'

'Don't be stupid,' Phil said. 'That'd be a waste of brain power. You can't work on a farm with Dad's qualifications. It'd be ridiculous.'

'Why not?' I said. 'They have to know all sorts of things about ... cows and pigs and tractors and stuff.'

'You're wasting your time talking to him,' Christine said, and of course Gillian had to join in. 'Waste of time,' she repeated, 'waste of time.' Then she started bleating.

35

'I only nudged her,' I said.

'Yes, with your elbow.'

'Oh, do stop bickering,' Mum said. 'Your father's a highly skilled specialist.'

'So's Jack,' I said. 'He can catch fish with his bare hands.'

'Oh yeah? Says who?'

I was bursting to tell Phil about the trout I'd caught, but what if Dad found out I was a poacher? I was determined to keep that a secret, even though it caused me actual physical pain to do so. But just as Phil was about to start jeering at me, Mum let me off the hook.

'Your brother's right,' she said. 'And so are you, Michael. It would be a waste of your father's education to be working with his hands; and in any case he'd never be able to learn everything those fellows know, not at his age. They've had a lifetime at it. Takes years to learn that sort of skill.'

Far from making me feel better, her answer heightened my anxiety. If I was going to learn everything Billy and Jack knew I'd surely better get started. The clock was ticking.

'Anyway, we'll be going back in a few weeks' time,' Mum said. 'It's not as if you'll never see your friends again, is it?'

I didn't answer her. It all seemed so unfair. We all loved being in the country, and we always felt fed up driving home from the farm. Even Petra seemed deflated, and slept on my knee all the way – which was good news, since it gave me a chance to tease all the sticky burrs out of her coat. As soon as we drove into the Avenue, however, she perked up and pressed her nose to the partly opened window and started whining, eager to get out and see what had been happening in the neighbourhood.

'Michael,' Dad said, getting out of the car and stretching, 'you take her for a walk while your mother gets tea on the table. And don't be long.'

I shoved my way past Christine and climbed out through the door, glad that I wouldn't be involved in unpacking the dirty laundry or

36

sweeping up the sand and bits of shell that had accumulated on the Traveller's seats. A man on a bicycle was coming down the road and Petra was off after him, barking and snapping at his heels.

'You wanna keep that dog of yours on a lead!' the man shouted as he pedalled furiously towards the main road.

As he drew away from Petra she came running back to me, her tongue out, grinning. I clipped the lead onto her collar.

'Let's go and see Spike,' I said, and at the very sound of his name Petra started to tug harder on the lead.

What she wanted was to go into my friend Tim's garden to see the rabbits. Tim's Dad kept a beautiful rock garden. He'd created a series of little hills and a small water feature powered by an electric pump. And, scattered amongst the shrubs and flowers, was his collection of weathervanes. I never knew what purpose they served, but some time later I was to be very grateful for them. I paused to look at the waterfall Tim's Dad had built, pulled Petra away and carried on towards the railway line to see whether Spike was at work.

Spike was the crossing-keeper. He seemed ancient to me, older even than Billy and Jack, with his snow-white hair and stubbly chin and blackened front teeth. He had a little brick-built cabin and he spent most of the day there, sitting in a tattered upholstered rocking-chair. He had a coal-fired stove to keep him warm, a big old kettle that was always steaming, a telephone and a pile of books – westerns mostly. All he had to do all day was open and close the gates when a train came through – which was about every hour or so on a busy day. Spike liked company. He must have been lonely, stuck out there with so little to do. He'd been in the war and was always telling us stories about his rescue from Dunkirk, his days in North Africa and Italy. That and his days as a fireman on the steam locos that thundered up and down the main line between York and London.

I must have been about seven when I first met Spike. It was a Saturday and we were playing down by the railway line, hanging around, waiting to catch a glimpse of the freight train that rattled through every morning about eleven, or maybe the fabled Deltic which, according to Phil, came by on holidays – not that I'd seen one yet. Sometimes in the summer we'd see the steam engine that pulled the trainspotters' special from Leeds to the coast. So was it any wonder we were drawn to the line? I knew that I shouldn't be there. Mum and Dad had always warned us to stay well away, but of course the prospect of watching the trains fly by was irresistible, all the more so when your big brother was telling you he had a new trick to show you. Up to that point Phil had always treated me as a baby. Most times I had to plead with him to let me follow him around, but as often as not he shook me off.

But this particular day he asked me, 'How many coins have you got?'

It was one of those dull days, with rain threatening, and nobody was about. For once in a while, he was at a loose end. I dug my hand into the pocket of my shorts and pulled out a sixpence, a penny and one of the new ten pence pieces.

'That'll do nicely,' he said.

'Where we going?' I asked.

'You'll see.'

To get to the line we had to cross a large field. It was planted up with barley – waist deep to me and just forming its seed-heads. We made our way around the edge, ploughing through the long grass and trampling the cow parsley. At the far side we could see the line, protected against intruders by a broken-down fence and a tangle of brambles. We fought our way through them, clambered over the fence, and stood looking at the sloping ballast, the sleepers and the shiny steel rails. Scarborough one way, York the other.

'Give us your money then,' Phil said.

I handed over the coins. 'What you going to do?' I asked.

He didn't answer me, just looked at his watch and said, 'Should be here in a couple of minutes.' He looked both ways, scrambled up the slope, laid the remains of my week's pocket money on the track and hurried back. 'Now we keep our heads down.'

The sun came out and warmed us as we crouched down below the level of the ballast. It was only when we heard the train approaching that I realised what was going on.

'Phil?' I said.

'Yeah what?'

'I'll still be able to spend my pocket money, won't I?'

'Yeah,' he said. 'Course you will.' He thought for a moment, then added, 'It'll go a lot further.'

I wasn't sure what he meant, but in any case whatever powers of reason I might have had were instantly derailed by the approach of the Class 37 engine, from this proximity a roaring monster of a thing with a blunt yellow nose. I knew it was a Class 37 because Phil said it was – and I knew better than to question his judgement. It was pulling a mixture of coal and oil wagons, a string of nondescript brown vans, a couple of long flats laden with steel girders – collected, he said, from Weaverthorpe – and of course a brake-van. I was fascinated by brake-vans, ever since I'd seen the guard leaning on the veranda, puffing on his pipe and waving to me one morning as we waited at Haxby level crossing gates with our bicycles. Much as I wanted a job like Billy and Jack's when I grew up, I also had a fancy for a life as a freight train guard. It seemed a leisured existence, and one of considerable status. However, there was no guard to wave at us this time, just a wisp of coal smoke coming from the chimney on the brake-van roof, and the train was soon disappearing in the direction of York.

Phil was on his feet, checking the line in both direction before climbing up the ballast once more.

'Can you see them?' I asked. He stood there for a moment, scanning the stone chippings before crouching down. 'Got the penny,' he said. 'And the ten pence. No sign of your tanner, though.'

He handed me the coins. I studied them carefully. The Queen's head on the penny was strangely distorted, the edges of the coin jagged, and it was almost twice its original size. The ten pence piece was a sort of elliptical shape and curved, but it gleamed in the sunlight. No doubt about it: it was an impressive result, but it had cost me.

'What about the sixpence you've lost?' I asked.

Phil surveyed the jumble of weeds and undergrowth that crowded the lineside, shrugged his shoulders and started to move off.

'It's your money. If you want it, you'd better start looking.'

I pushed my way a few feet into the brambles, scratching my arms as I did so. Beneath my feet was a mat of dead grass and bits of litter. I felt the weight of the two squashed coins in my pocket, decided that I'd better cut my losses, and hurried after my brother. He was already halfway to the crossing-keeper's cabin.

'Now then, boys. What you been up to?' Spike was spooning sugar into a freshly made mug of tea. Behind him on a little gas ring a kettle was simmering. 'Not putting coins on the line, I hope.'

'N-no!' I said. I may have been not quite seven years old, but I knew it was a good idea to deny anything any adult accused me of.

'Go on, show him.' Phil was prodding me with his forefinger, pointing at my pocket. I looked at him, then at Spike, who was grinning at me, exposing his blackened teeth.

'Don't worry, lad. I won't shop you. Boys have been doing that since dinosaurs trod the Earth,' he said. 'It's as natural as breathing. Go on, let me have a look.'

I took the coins out of my pocket and handed them to him.

'Why,' he said, 'they're a couple of beauties, aren't they? A real treasure.' He handed them back. 'And what's your name, eh?'

'John,' I said. Phil looked at me, his mouth hanging open. But before he could correct me, Spike carried on. 'Well John, young fellow-me-lad, just you take care of yourself, you hear?' Then he turned to Phil. 'You lads going to stop and have a bit of cake with me?'

I looked at Phil. Were we allowed? Was this like taking sweets from a stranger?

'Sure,' he said. Spike was already opening up a big Oxo tin and peeling the grease-proof paper off a slab of rich fruit cake. 'My missus,' he said. 'Doesn't want me to starve, does she?'

We sat against the outside wall of the cabin and ate the cake while Spike perched on a metal-framed chair, supped his tea and told us how he'd escaped from Dunkirk, wading into the icy water as the bombs fell around him and clambering aboard a cabin cruiser that had sailed all the way from Yarmouth. 'Aye,' he said, 'England's finest moment.' And then he put his mug down on the ground, grinned and said, 'or so they told us.'

A few minutes later Phil looked at his watch and said we ought to be going.

'Aye,' Spike said, 'drop in again, you lads.' He looked at the sky where a dark cloud was covering the sun. 'Better hurry up before the weather changes,' he said. Then he looked at me. 'And you look after yourself, young John.'

'Don't worry,' Phil said. 'He'll be okay with me.' As we made our way back across the field he asked, 'What's all this John business then?'

'That's what I want to be called,' I said.

'What's wrong with Michael?'

The truth was, I'd been watching a lot of cowboy films on the telly, and as soon as I saw John Wayne I decided that that was the kind of man I'd like to grow up to be. And I'd take his name too. And once I'd thought that, it was a short step to deciding that Michael was a sissy sort of name.

'I don't like Michael,' I said. 'It makes people call you Mickey, and then every time people say they're taking the mickey I feel sort of – funny. Anyway, it sounds like a girl's name.'

Phil thought for a moment, then said, 'Maybe it does and maybe it doesn't. But I tell you what.'

'What?'

'Getting a new name isn't going to stop you being a big girl's blouse.' And with that he shoved me over and ran off across the field.

I picked myself up and chased after him. One day, I swore to myself, I would get revenge. Just because he was taller than me he thought he could do as he liked. But one day … one day he'd stop growing and I'd carry on, and then he'd better watch out. I hurried on around the hedge-side. I'd almost caught up with him when I spotted something strange in a neighbouring field. It was a huge yellow machine with caterpillar tracks, a vertical exhaust and a curved, shiny, steel blade on the front, and it was chugging its way across land that had been lying fallow for as long as we could remember – just the occasional horse or two tied up by travellers passing through.

Phil had seen it too. He'd stopped to stare, same as I had.

'What is it?' I asked.

We both stood there and watched it ploughing the top off the field and piling the earth up.

'Wow, that's a bulldozer! And a big one,' he said. 'C'mon, let's go and have a look.'

It was the biggest, most exciting machine I'd ever seen. The noise it made – and the cloud of dark smoke that spewed into the afternoon sky – was thrilling. It had a glass cab, and through the glass I could make out a man in a peaked cap, a cigarette in his mouth, pulling levers as he manoeuvred the big beast backwards and forwards. Here was yet another job I could have when I grew up. The world seemed full of exciting opportunities – but which one to take? We stood and watched it work to and fro, piling up the earth in a huge mound, until we realised that it had come on to rain and we were getting wet. We hurried home. It would soon be time for tea, after we'd sat and watched our favourite TV show, The Goodies.

'Dad, Mum!' I said as we burst in through the back door. 'Guess what we've seen? A giant bulldozer. It's in the field. You want to see it, it's fantastic.'

Dad was deep in his Evening Press. He seemed unmoved. 'I see,' he murmured, 'so they've started, have they?'

That wasn't good enough for me. I wanted a reaction. 'Mum, Mum!' I shouted. 'There's this giant bulldozer, with smoke coming out of its chimney. It's fantastic. It's in the field. Do you think I could be a bulldozer driver when I grow up?'

'Yes, Michael, I heard you the first time. Now go and wash your hands. I don't know how you get them so dirty.'

I hurried off to the sink, wondering whether she meant yes, I could be a dozer driver, or yes, she knew about it. That was the thing with adults, it seemed to me. You never really knew what they meant.

We children watched our show, after which it was teatime. I brought the subject up once more, and this time Mum explained. 'There's been talk of them building a housing estate over there for a long time. It sounds as though it's finally going to happen.'

'Yes,' Dad said, folding his paper and putting in his hip pocket before taking his seat, 'the inexorable march of the city. It'll swallow the village up before long. And there's not a lot we can do about it, I'm afraid.'

He didn't say anything else, but I could tell he wasn't happy. Mum had bought kippers for tea, one of his favourites, but he ate almost in silence. And after we'd got down, and Christine and I had gone to do the dishes, he disappeared into his shed. He spent a lot of time out there, and at that age I didn't really know what he was up to – apart from maintaining the car. Neither did any of us know, at the time, that this was going to be good news for all us before too long.

Meanwhile our neighbours had evidently got to hear what was going on. More importantly, their children had got wind of it too. Over the next few evenings, as the field started filling up with piles of sand

and gravel, hills of topsoil, stacks of assorted bricks and timber, as well as rows of concrete pipes, and a whole range of yellow-painted machinery, so all the children within a mile or two were drawn to the site like bees to a honey-pot. The contractors fenced it off. Of course they did. But while they may have kept out the local villains who cruised around the perimeter in their vans and trucks eyeing up the materials on display, we kids were in under the fence like so many rabbits, turning the place into our very own adventure playground.

Over that summer we climbed the sand-piles and tobogganed down them on scraps of plywood. We dared each other to climb the ladders that were left lying against the sides of half-built houses, and walked around the scaffold-boards shouting to each other and staging mock battles between cowboys and Indians, British and German soldiers, or Robin Hood and the Sheriff of Nottingham, depending on what TV programmes we'd been watching, or what comics we'd been reading at the time.

One sultry August evening we rigged up a diving board and took turns to jump off it into a large tank of water, and all around the neighbourhood irate mothers scolded their offspring for coming home soaked to the skin, while their grinning, dripping kids asked if they could be excused washing – seeing that they'd already had a dip.

In all the many evenings we played over there I don't recall seeing a single security guard patrolling the site. Perhaps they only came on duty at nightfall. Perhaps it was a more innocent age. The only aggravation we got was an occasional shout from a passing dog-walker who waved a stick and threatened to call the police. But whether they did or not we never found out. We certainly never saw the boys in blue.

Just when we thought life couldn't get much more exciting, news reached our ears that it could indeed. The new estate was being built by Barratts. We all knew who Barratts were: they were the ones who advertised on the telly. We loved those adverts almost as much as we loved the programmes they interrupted. What could be more thrilling than seeing Patrick Allen parachute from a helicopter before it smashed through a fake wall, uttering the immortal catchphrase 'Now that's a breakthrough!'

I loved Patrick Allen. When I wasn't dreaming of being John Wayne, this was the man I aspired to be. He seemed to me a combination of my cowboy hero, my caterpillar driver and my freight train guard, with a dash of James Bond and Spiderman thrown in. What's more, he was English, which pleased Dad. What a life it must be, I thought, riding around the countryside in a helicopter. And now the news leaked out that the great man was going to drop in on us. I say it leaked; in fact it was advertised on posters all around the site which was now nearing completion, with the flags flying and the show-house open to potential buyers.

It may have spelled the end of a glorious summer of fun and adventure, but what did we care when we heard that the man from Barratts was going to arrive, in his helicopter, on the new estate, our estate? As if that wasn't enough excitement, The Goodies, whose show we watched religiously, were going to show up on their bicycle-made-for-three.

If I'd been a year or two older I might have had the good sense to keep my mouth shut about all this, but at that age there was no way I could contain my excitement.

'Mum, Dad, Mum, Dad! You'll never guess!' I burst out as I hurtled in through the back door, only to be stopped in my tracks by Mum, a mop in her hand, standing on a square of newspaper with a bucket of soapy water beside her.

'Not in your muddy shoes!' she shouted. 'Out! This minute! Do you hear me?'

I used to hate that, the way adults always seemed determined to take the wind out of your sails. Why were they so ... calm, so boring? Here was I, bearing the most thrilling news Park Avenue had ever heard, and all my Mum seemed to care about was a bit of mud on my shoes.

'Now then,' she said, after she finally gave me the all-clear to tiptoe across her polished floor and into the back sitting-room, 'what's all the excitement about this time?'

'It's the Goodies,' I said.

'And the man from the Barratts advert,' Phil added. Even he was getting wound up now.

'Yes? What about them?' Dad had put down his paper and narrowed his eyes – which I knew wasn't good news. It was his 'persuade me' look.

'They're coming to the new estate and they'll be giving out sweets and things, and we'll be on the telly, and – '

'No we won't.' Phil might have been getting into it, but he wasn't getting carried away. 'It won't be on the telly, but it's going to be dead good. Can we go?'

'And when is this?' Mum asked.

'Saturday afternoon,' Phil said.

'I don't know,' she said, casting a glance at Dad.

Dad looked us up and down.

'I don't want you two going over there. It's too far from home. You could easily get lost.'

I looked at Phil. Didn't they realise we'd been playing over on the site for weeks and weeks, that we knew our way there and back blindfolded?

'No,' Dad continued, 'I don't like the sound of it.'

After tea that night Phil and I held a whispered conversation in the back garden.

'Don't worry,' he said. 'They'll never know.'

'Never know what?'

He tutted impatiently. 'If we go to the estate on Saturday.'

'You mean …?'

'Sure. So long as we get back in time for tea. Who's to say where we've been?' And then he grabbed me by the shoulders. 'But listen.'

'I'm listening.'

'I don't want you saying a word about this to anyone – especially not the girls, you hear?'

I swore I'd keep my mouth shut. Not only was I thrilled to think that my dream would come true, but here I was hatching a plan with my big brother. It was as if I was his side-kick, and that felt extra good.

The week that followed seemed to last a month. Longer than that. It was like waiting for Christmas, or you birthday. Saturday seemed so far distant that I struggled to believe it would ever arrive. I compiled a chart and hid it under my mattress. That was at night. In the daytime I rolled it up, shoved it up my shirt and took it to school with me. I kept it pinned to the underside of my desk lid, and every so often I'd open it up and have a quick check, almost as if I expected another day to have passed. I had them all written in big block capital letters. Monday, Tuesday, Wednesday, Thursday, Friday ... The Great Day Itself. But waiting for the first day to pass took too long. It was more than I could stand. I re-drafted it, dividing each day into sections. Tuesday morning, dinner, Tuesday afternoon, tea, Tuesday night. Finally, I tore a huge sheet off a roll of old wallpaper I found under the stairs and started again. Now every day was sub-divided into twenty-four hours.

'What you bothering with that for?'

Phil was allowed up a full half-hour later than me, and I'd always try and stay awake to hear what had happened in the TV show I'd been watching when Mum called me through to get ready for bed. When he came up that night he found me crouched on the floor, waiting for the big hand to reach the twelve on the Thunderbirds alarm clock – at which point I scored through another hour with a flourish.

'Because,' I explained, 'a day takes ages and ages.'

'Yeah, but – every hour?'

Phil didn't get it, and it was my task to explain it to him.

'See, when I get up in the morning,' I said, 'it's great. I get to wipe out a whole load of hours at once.'

Somehow the week made its tortuous way to the end. Saturday morning was finally here and I could take my felt-tip pen and cross out another ten hours. By the time I'd done my weekly jobs and earned my twenty pence pocket money – four bob in Dad's language – it would be almost time to make our pilgrimage across the field where we would witness the most wonderful event of my young life so far.

Everything was in place for a great afternoon. The sun was out, we'd been across to the shop where I spent a slice of my pocket money on an ice-cream and a bag of salt-and-vinegar crisps. By the time I'd scoffed them and we'd made our way to the estate it was barely fifteen minutes before the scheduled arrival of the TV stars. People were walking in from all directions. Hordes of them. There were knots of youths, families, gaggles of kids – and a few bemused motorists crawling through the village in first gear. As we entered the estate on the newly tarmac'd road we saw a York Evening Press van, a couple of ice-cream vendors and a mobile chippy; there was even a police car parked beside the show house. The man from the Press had a camera round his neck and was on one knee, photographing the crowds. I tried to drag Phil over.

'Come on, we can be in the paper,' I said, running a hand through my hair and standing there with a big grin on my face.

'Never mind that,' Phil said. 'Let's get a move on or we'll miss him.'

But I waited for the camera to click before following him. We shoved our way through the tightly packed crowd of people gathered around the spot where our man was to land. They stood in silent expectation, and after a while we heard a murmur spread through them, a murmur that grew into a great long 'Aaa-ah!' Everybody was craning their necks, scanning the skies – and there, coming in over the roof-tops was the Barratts helicopter. It looked simply huge, and the way it hovered, almost perfectly still, all but took my breath away.

'Wow! There he is!'

I hurled myself forward and wormed my way through the crush. I heard Phil call after me to wait for him. I knew he'd told me not to lose sight of him, but the thought of seeing Patrick Allen descending from the heavens was too much. I squeezed between a couple of old ladies and found myself up against a rope with the landing-spot in front of me. The air was filled with the sound of rotor blades whirring. Great gusts of wind were blowing dust in our eyes. Women were hanging onto their skirts and hats. And then the magic moment: our craggy-faced hero in his grey suit and wearing his headphones, stepping deftly from the chopper and waving to the multitude as he landed neatly on his feet.

To tell the truth, it all got a bit boring after that. People started making speeches. Some fellow in a suit took over and began yapping about mortgages and percentages. I looked around, wondering where Phil had got to. Maybe he'd gone to see the Goodies.

It's a strange thing, being lost. I mean when you're little. I suppose I can only speak for myself, but since I was the kind of child who couldn't resist wandering off alone, I managed to get lost a number of times – and I always remember the feeling. One minute the world is perfectly normal. Yes, you're surrounded by strangers, but you don't see them as strangers when you're with someone close to you – your Dad, your Mum, your big brother. But once I realised that Phil wasn't there – that I'd lost him – I suddenly saw all those faces around me as what they were: people I didn't know. People I'd never seen before. People who looked right through me and took no notice of one more little boy. Within a few moments the whole world had turned into a strange and frightening place. I seem to remember crying, trying to fight my way out from the crowd. Next thing I remember I was in the open and some helpful person was putting an arm around me and asking me what was wrong; but that frightened me even more and I wrestled myself free and ran off as fast as I could. Of course, I had no idea what direction I was running in. While we had got to know our way around the building site over the summer, so many changes had taken place so suddenly during the last couple of weeks, with people moving into the new houses, with lawns being laid and trees planted and cars appearing where there had previously been sand-heaps and site-huts. Now I was hopelessly at sea – and, without realising it, getting deeper and deeper into trouble.

I'd managed to escape the crowds, but I was on a road I'd never been down before, lined with houses that looked unfamiliar. There was a gang of boys standing looking at me, older boys. One of them shouted something. Another threw a stone. A dog barked. I turned and headed off in a new direction, towards a row of shops. But they weren't our shops – not the newsagent I'd walk to with Dad, nor the confectioners I'd ridden my bike to that very morning to agonise over flying saucers, black-jacks and Bazooka bubble-gum. I stood there, fighting back tears, a horrible trembling sensation overtaking me.

And then something wonderful happened. I saw a boy I recognised from my class at school. He was coming out of a sweet-shop – and he was with his mother. I ran over to him and blurted out, 'How do I get to Park Avenue? I went to see the helicopter and I don't know my way home.'

The boy's mother took my hand and led me back along the road.

'You're lucky you found us,' she said. 'Goodness knows where you might have ended up. Now, Park Avenue, did you say?'

'Yes,' I sniffed.

'And what number is it?'

We must have walked for a mile or so before I started to recognise where we were. The kind lady took me all the way to our front door and handed me over to Mum. She was relieved to see me, of course; but after she'd hugged me and thanked my rescuer and seen her on her way, she hit the roof.

'And where exactly have you been to?'

'I been playing in the park.'

'Who with?'

'Just some of my friends.'

'And what about your brother, eh? Where's he? Answer me.'

I had no idea where Phil was, of course. The last I'd seen of him he was off in search of the Goodies. As I stood there, not knowing whether to come clean or keep up the pretence, she must have realised I was holding back.

'You've been over at the estate, haven't you? After what your father said.'

'No,' I whined. 'I was playing cricket, in the park.'

Behind me, Christine laughed. 'I bet he has,' she said.

'You keep out of this!' I shouted.

Mum ignored the sideshow. 'And what about that brother of yours? Where's he?'

'I don't know.'

That brother of mine didn't show up for another hour. And when he did he was mightily distressed. He really thought he'd lost me for good, and arrived at the door in tears. Then he saw me, sitting there eating my tea and doing my best not to grin at him. He was in trouble, of course, for being late, but with a crafty wink he made me understand that we were not to admit to anything.

We'd got away with it. When we went to bed that night we both heaved exaggerated sighs of relief, then laughed until we had to bury our heads in our pillows to stifle the row.

Not a word was said about the affair over the rest of the weekend. We'd cracked it. Got away with it. What a good feeling it was.

Then came Monday evening. Mum was in the kitchen making tea. Dad was in his easy chair scanning the paper. We kids were all sitting in front of the television, straining to hear what was being said. Dad would only let us watch it when he was in the room if we turned the sound way down so that he didn't have to hear it. Suddenly, as he turned a page he froze. He gave out a long low sort of sighing noise, then inhaled deeply. Rising from his chair he switched off the telly, told the girls to go to the kitchen and help Mum, then turned to address me and Phil.

'Right, you two. You have some explaining to do.'

I remember starting to shake. There was no doubt what this was about. As far as I could remember I'd done nothing else that could've provoked such a reaction. But how had he found out?

As Dad marched towards me I staggered backwards until my rear end was pressing against the living room wall. I had my eyes shut.

'Just what … is the meaning of this? Hm?'

I opened my eyes, just a crack. I wasn't looking at Dad but at the Evening Press. As the page came into focus I saw the picture. A crowd of people grinning at the camera, and there, right slap-bang in the middle, waving, face cracked by a huge grin: me.

Dad lowered the paper and stood there, frowning at me. 'Care to explain?' he asked.

I can't remember what the punishment was, but knowing Dad I suspect it would have 'fitted the crime'. Most likely it was the most exquisite torture he could inflict on me: staying inside the house or garden for the next week. No trips to the park to play cricket with my mates; no walks down to the railway line to listen to Spike's war stories; no expeditions down to the beck to fish or join the boys for a quick dip.

But you know what? It was worth it.

Bows and Arrows

When I think back to my childhood it seems to me that I was a little boy with a very inquisitive streak. I was always exploring, always investigating, always taking things apart. You'd think that adults would approve of that, that they'd want to bring out the potential mechanic, or inventor, in me – my practical side. I mean, James Watt must have started somewhere. But they couldn't see it. Half the time they thought I was nothing but a nuisance – and didn't hesitate to tell me so.

'Questions, questions, questions,' they said. 'Always asking questions.'

And, when I started peering into the back of the telly, or the fridge, or upending the vacuum cleaner, it was, 'Leave that thing alone!' Or, if they'd left it too late, 'Now put it back together – and woe betide you if it doesn't work.'

What people objected to most of all was when my restless, enquiring mind took me into the fields, down along the beck, across to the railway line, or into Dad's workshops. But that's what I liked best, being out of the house.

I couldn't stand being confined indoors, especially not if that meant the classroom. In school, I had little interest in what was written on the blackboard – or in anything that didn't make loud noises, didn't move quickly, didn't look as though it might explode. So why would I be interested in all that reading, writing and arithmetic? Bo-ring!

And so I looked out of the window. The world out there seemed so much more interesting. There were birds building nests, planes flying by, the noise of distant traffic. There was the ever-changing weather, always catching my attention. And there were people doing interesting things. Sometimes, for instance, a coal lorry would come into the yard and I'd see men with blackened faces humping sacks of coke across the playground, blokes who whistled and chewed gum and gave you the thumbs-up if they caught sight of you. How come none of our teachers did that? I'd have been far more likely to listen to them if they'd been able to raise one eyebrow and wink at the same time, like the milkman did, or put a piece of string in their mouth and bring it out knotted, like the caretaker, standing outside the boiler-house during playtime and performing conjuring tricks for us. Why were teachers so dull?

The thing was, I wasn't daft. I could've been up near the top of the form if I'd been interested. If only they'd had lessons about toy guns – and how they worked; or bikes – and how to make them go faster; or how to build soap-box carts that didn't fall apart every time you crashed; or how to bake a conker without it bursting open. And what about fireworks? I asked the question in class one time. We were being taught about the Gunpowder Plot, and of course I was all ears. The idea that somebody back in ancient times had had the bright idea of blowing up Parliament – wow, that was my kind of history. I put my hand up and shouted, 'Miss, Miss, Miss!'

'There's only one teacher in the room, Michael, so one "Miss" is perfectly adequate. Now, what is it you want to ask?'

'You know every Christmas, Miss, when we all make a cracker to take home?'

'Ye-es.' I could tell by the way she answered that she was on her guard. I don't think she really approved of us making crackers. It was far too much fun.

'Well, Miss, seeing as it's Guy Fawkes next week, why don't we get some gunpowder and have an experiment and see who can make the best banger, Miss?'

'Michael, we do not come to school to learn how to make explosives.'

'Why not, Miss? I mean, it would help us understand old Guy Fawkes, wouldn't it?' It seemed a fair question to me, but half the class groaned, and the other half laughed.

'Michael Pannett, we prefer not to play around with gunpowder for two reasons. One, because it's a lethal substance, and two, because we have better things to do.'

I thought for a moment, trying to imagine something better than making bangers and rockets. I soon gave that up as a dead loss, but I wasn't beaten; not yet. I was like a dog with a bone.

'But Miss,' I said, 'in factories and that … I mean, whoever makes the fireworks must be an expert. They must have learned all about explosions and that before they got the job. Otherwise there wouldn't be any fireworks, would there?'

I really thought I'd got her there, but one thing I was to learn over the years was that teachers always have an answer for you.

'You are very likely correct, Michael, but I don't think the person in question would have learned his skills at New Earswick Primary. Now, let's get back to the story of Mister Guy Fawkes, shall we? And then after break we can carry on sticking those autumn leaves in our books.'

Sticking leaves in a book. Now where was the fun in that? It was all books – that and copying from the blackboard. I had little interest in reading back them. Comics, yes. Actual books, no. So when I couldn't look out of the window I just got bored – until I got to twelve or thirteen and discovered girls, that is. When it came to girls I would be keen as mustard. And a fast learner, always willing to do a spot of homework. But that was in the future. When I was seven, eight, nine all I wanted was to be outside, learning about the world, experimenting. Like when we went on those wonderful trips to Staintondale. Now that was my kind of education. There was always something to learn over there.

Jack had taught me to tickle trout. Later he'd teach me about fly-fishing, something that still interests me to this day. But Jack wasn't my only tutor. Billy, with his grubby old flat hat and brown corduroy trousers, also had a lot to teach me. He was different in his approach, though. Whereas Jack would offer to teach you something you'd never thought about, Billy would wait till he saw you wrestling with a particular problem – as he did one summer's morning when he found me out in the yard trying to make the best of a bad job.

It had all started with cowboys and Indians. Mum had confiscated my six-gun when I charged it with a double dose of percussion caps, stole up behind her and pulled the trigger, causing her to drop an entire basket of clean washing in a puddle.

Mum was angry, very angry indeed. At first she threatened to make me re-do the entire wash. Then she remembered the time I'd bleached my best trousers to get them clean, and changed her mind. Instead, she took away my most prized possession, and the red belt and holster for good measure, and said I might get it back when I'd learned my lesson. What's more, I would miss the morning's outing to Bempton Cliffs to look at the puffins. If that didn't teach me a lesson, nothing would. When she suggested that Doris might find me some work around the kitchen I took it as a clear signal that I should stay in the yard, and out of sight if possible.

I put a brave face on it. I didn't want to see any stupid puffins anyway, I told myself. And off they went, leaving me with Petra. There was no way they'd take her bird-watching.

For a while I mooched about the yard. Billy and Jack had both gone out into the fields. I sat in the sun thinking about cowboys. Then I spotted Gillian's skipping rope that she'd abandoned as she hurried into the car with the others. I picked it up, tied it at one end to make a slip-knot, and settled down to see whether I could make a lasso. Maybe I could throw a loop over Petra, the way my cowboy heroes lassoed runaway cows. She was very obliging about it: just sat there, head on one side, and waited patiently as I threw the rope at her, time after time, with the same result. Even when I managed to land it on top of her head it still flopped at her feet in a hopeless tangle.

Just when I was about to give it up, I heard the tractor coming up the lane and into the yard. Billy drove it up to the barn, got out and stood under the eaves, eyeing the pigeons that were always gathered there, drawn by the spilled corn and chicken-feed.

'Flaming birds,' I heard him say. 'If I had my way I'd poison the lot of 'em.'

I tried to throw my rope a couple more times, no more successfully than before. Billy had one foot up on a big old log that stood by the barn door. He seemed to be re-threading a lace. The log was more like a tree-stump, really. It had been there since the old days, according to him and Jack, when the three aunties were little and used to hop up on it in order to mount a horse. He finished what he was doing, then came across to where I was standing. He didn't say anything, just took the rope in his hand, and ran it through his fingers. Finally he spoke.

'You'll never throw a loop with this, young Michael.'

'What, am I doing something wrong?'

Billy pushed his flat hat back and rubbed his forehead. 'Why,' he said, 'it's not you; it's your rope. It's the wrong sort.'

'Oh,' I said, and waited for him to tell me more. Billy was what you'd call deliberate. Slow and deliberate. He always thought before he spoke, and he never hurried anything. 'Them cowboys,' he continued, 'they had what they call rawhide. That's leather as hasn't been tanned. Real tough, it is.' He handed me the rope, undid the buckle on his belt and pulled it out, careful to stop his leather sheath dropping on the ground. He always wore a belt, and with it the short, dark brown sheath with a brass rivet at the bottom. He worked the belt into a loop and held it for me to see. 'A cowboy rope's more like this,' he said. 'What you've got there is way too limp. You mek a rope of rawhide and it's stiff as this belt – stiff as a length of a wire cable. You mek a rope out of this and it holds its shape, d'you see?'

I did. I stood there, fully expecting him to take me in the shed and conjure up just such a length of rawhide as he was talking about. But he didn't. Instead, he looked at me and shook his head. 'I'm afraid you're wasting your time with that thing and you may as well know it.'

I let the rope drop to the ground. 'I wanted to be a proper cowboy,' I sniffed. 'And lasso things.'

'I know,' Billy said, picking the rope up once more and looping it over his forearm. 'I know just how you feel. Same as me and Jack did when we were growing up in Cloughton. We were crazy about cowboys – aye, and Indians too.'

'You were?' Looking at old Billy I couldn't imagine him racing around the yard playing cowboys and Indians.

'Aye, every time t'owd travelling cinema came through we got a proper dose of wild west fever. All on us lads.'

'A travelling cinema,' I said, trying to imagine such a thing. When Mum and Dad took us to the flicks we went into York – to the ABC or the Odeon. But a travelling cinema. All I could think of was the fish-and-chip van that Mum used to tell us about, the one which came around when she was a lass. Maybe that's what Billy meant, a van that they all crammed into to watch the films – like the mobile library that came to Staintondale once a week.

Billy sighed and said, 'It were just a van, like. They'd come round the villages every so often and tek over the old church hall or mebbe t'library. Throw up a big old bed-sheet at one end and set up the projector at t'other on a wooden table, with rows of chairs in between and put t'first reel on.' He was grinning as he remembered. 'And woe betide anyone who stood up and blocked out the light. We'd all whistle and shout till he sat down again.'

We'd wandered over toward the barn by this time and Billy had sat himself down on the old tree-stump.

'Aye, and when the sheriff went stalking them baddies and we spotted them hiding we'd all shout out, "Look out, they're over there! Behind the rock!"' He kept chuckling as he reminisced. 'Aye, it was quite a do when t'travelling picture show came around.' As he spoke he coiled the skipping rope, tighter this time. Then he paused and said, 'We used to carve toy guns, out of wood – aye, and we made lassos, just like you was doing. And you know what, young Michael?'

'No, what?'

He laughed. 'We couldn't mek 'em work neither.' Then he leaned forward and winked at me and said, 'But d'you know what we did do? Eh? Shall I tell you?'

'What?' I was all ears now.

'We learned how to mek bows and arrows,' he said, and sat up straight and put his hands on his knees. 'Now then. How'd you like that, eh? To be an Indian, instead of a cowboy? D'you want me to show you? It's just as much fun.'

'Wow!' I said. 'You bet.'

'Right, we'll gather up a tool or two, shall we, and off to t'woods.'

I followed him into the workshop where he picked up a beautiful steel knife with a wooden handle and slid it into the sheath on his belt. Then he reached up to the collection of saws and handed me one.

'You tek the bow-saw, lad. And be careful,' he added. He chuckled gently as he showed me how to carry it over my shoulder with the teeth behind me and the smooth metal handle to the front. 'Them teeth used to belong a shark,' he said.

Naturally I believed him, and thought about it all the way out of the yard and down the lane that led to the woods, wondering how they'd caught the shark and why the teeth weren't white like anybody else's. And when it finally occurred to me that he might have been making it up I tightened my grip on the bow-saw and thought about what a brilliant idea it was to have a special saw for making bows with.

Instead of going into the woods and along the path that led down to the Wyke, we climbed over a rickety wooden style and followed the edge of a field, beside a tall hedge. There was a stiff breeze blowing, and the sea, which we could see beyond a bank of gorse-bushes, was flecked with white-caps.

'Now then, young Michael, d'you know what these are?' Billy was leaning over a sagging strand of wire. He had hold of a tall sapling of some sort and was pulling it towards us. 'Come on, lad, what kind of tree's this? Don't tell me you don't know.'

I shook my head. I knew what a conker tree was like, and a holly tree, but not a lot else.

'Why, it's a hazel, lad. If you look carefully you'll see a few nuts. Here y'are, here's some – see?' He'd tugged at one of the slender branches and held it in front of me.

Standing on my tiptoes I could just see a cluster of pale green nuts. 'Can we eat them?' I asked, reaching out to grab at them.

He laughed and let the branch spring back to where it belonged. 'Not until t'autumn,' he said. 'And only if t'squirrels and birds leave you a few. Anyway, that's not what we're after just now, is it? We're after mekking you a sturdy bow, to go hunting with.' As he spoke he reached out and grabbed another sapling and bent it down towards where I could get my hand around it. 'Now then,' he said, 'you keep hold on it, and I'll saw off what we need. See how nice and springy it is?'

'Yes,' I said. 'I do.'

'Well, that's where you get the power from.' I still wasn't sure what he meant but I did as I was told and held tight while he started sawing. With the moist saw-dust falling like snow, I breathed deep to catch the sweet smell of the sap. Half a dozen strokes and he was through, and now I was holding the felled sapling across my knee while he lopped off the top and threaded the unwanted foliage through the hedge and out of sight.

'Right,' he said, 'that's your bow. Let's go and find some willow wood, shall we? No good having a bow without any arrows, is it now?'

We crossed the field – a sheep pasture it was, although most of the sheep were gathered at the other end of it. Billy loped along in front while I hurried behind him with our length of hazel wood. It was mostly downhill, and it led to a little beck that formed the boundary.

There was a thicket of trees growing there, nondescript trees that formed a waving green barrier.

'Willows,' he said. 'Just the job, lad.'

Suddenly Billy was out of sight. I peered over the edge of the steep bank. All I could see were the branches twitching this way and that and the leaves fluttering. Then he was clambering up the bank with his right arm wrapped around a bundle of long thin canes. He threw them onto the grass. They were smooth and straight with just a few leaves on them – at the tip.

'Now,' he said, sitting down beside them and wiping his forehead with a large red handkerchief, 'you go and cut some more.'

I needed no further invitation. I took his knife and slithered down into the tangle of young willows. The sharp steel blade cut through the young shoots easily, and I quickly had another stack to carry up to Billy, who lay on his back watching the clouds go by.

'Good lad,' he said, eyeing the neat pile. 'I reckon that'll do us for now. It's time for some refreshment, don't you think so lad?' With that he reached into his pocket and pulled out a stick of rock. 'I've been saving this for you lot,' he said. 'Bought four of them in Filey. Last summer, it was.'

We sat there for some time in the sunshine. I chewed on the rock while Billy started sorting through the lengths of willow we'd collected, discarding the odd crooked one, one or two that he considered too green, and some that were too thin or too thick.

'Thing with arrows,' he said, 'they want to be just right, else they won't fly straight.'

Then he dug deep in the pocket of his brown corduroy trousers, pulled out a length of twine and tied up the ones he'd selected.

'There,' he said, 'twenty arrows – once they're trimmed and sharpened. We need to peel the bark off before it dries out as well. But I'll tell you summat else we need to get.'

'Feathers,' I said. 'We need some feathers to put in the end, don't we?'

He slapped his knee and laughed. 'By golly, there's no flies on you, lad. Feathers it is. And I'll tell you where we'll start. In the henhouse, eh?' Then he added, 'But what I was going to say was, string. You'll want some strong waxed twine for your bow, won't you?' He nudged me, then got slowly to his feet.

Back at the yard, Billy and I went into the shed. There I started peeling the bark off. The wood underneath was smooth, white and slick, sweet-smelling too. As I peeled, he took them from me one by one, rubbed them dry on his trousers and trimmed them, whittling a sharp point on one end, and making a cut in the other – for the feathers, he said. Meanwhile, I looked around to make sure none of the aunties were about, slipped into the potting shed and came out with a ball of strong twine. Then the pair of us went into the chicken-run in search of feathers – or tried to. The old cockerel didn't welcome visitors, and was at our ankles, pecking away, as soon as we opened the little wire-mesh gate and ducked inside.

'Go on wi' you!' Billy shouted. 'You long streak of useless gristle.'

He aimed a kick at the grubby white bird and missed, stifling a swearword as he skidded on a patch of poop and almost lost his footing.

'You go inside, lad,' he told me. 'Go on, grab some feathers and I'll keep this little – blighter at arm's length. Always been a bad-tempered so-and-so, and I tell you what.' He paused and narrowed his eyes. 'One of these days, I'll have him.' And with that he bent down, picked up a lump of clay and hurled it at the indignant cockerel. 'Aye, in a pot wi' a few leeks and some shallots.'

It was dark inside the henhouse, and warm. There was a sharp smell of ammonia. I knew all about ammonia, from the time I'd found a bottle in Mum's cleaning drawer and took a deep sniff of it. It nearly took the top of my head off. Along one side of the house was a series of nestboxes, and four or five plump brown hens sitting there, blinking at me from their beds of clean straw. Across the middle of the floor was a low bar, nailed onto four round logs and all covered in dried poop. That was their perch, where they roosted at night. I'd seen them when I went for the eggs on an evening. In the corners was a little drift of feathers. I scooped up a double handful and took them outside to see Billy, likewise crouched, but face to face with the irate rooster.

'I'm telling you, your days are numbered,' he muttered through clenched teeth. 'Them hens can do just as well without you, you know.' Then he turned to me and grinned. 'Why, you've enough feathers there to make a war bonnet too. Come along, lad, let's get weaving, shall we?'

We sat outside, Billy on the old tree-stump, me on an upturned bucket.

'Been a few years since I turned me hand to this,' he said, as he picked out the best of the feathers and trimmed them with his knife, before slotting them into the ends of the arrows where he'd made the little nick earlier. 'But it's like riding a bicycle,' he said. 'Once you've learned it you never forget.' He handed me an arrow. 'Time for you to have a go,' he said, and watched as I copied what he'd done.

With the arrows all lined up, some with brown feathers, others with white, we set about finishing the bow.

'First we cut a notch around it at this end,' Billy said. 'Like a groove, d'you see? That's for t'string to sit in. I'll do one, so's you get the idea, then you do the other end.' I did as he showed me, then stood in the shed and watched as he split the wood at either end, wet the string, wound it several times around the end of the bow, then slid his knife into the split to open it up, slipped the string through and removed the knife, allowing the wood to tighten around it.

'Now, this is the important part,' he said. 'This is where we mek it good and tight.'

And saying that he grunted, pulled hard on the string, so bending the stave of hazel till it made a sort of D shape. Then he let it slip into the notch at the far end before winding it swiftly round and round in the groove we'd cut.

'Now we tie a little knot – like so – and Bob's your uncle.'

He took the bow in his left hand, raised it to shoulder level, pulled on the string with two fingers of his right and let go. It made a satisfying sort of 'thwunk'.

'Here,' he said, handing me the bow, 'you have a go.'

It took all my strength to do as he had done, but what a good feeling it was. All that power, with the arc of the bow quivering as I cranked up the tension.

'Now,' he said, 'let's see if we can mek these arrows fly, shall we?'

With that he took one from the pile, carefully slotted the end of it onto the newly fitted bow-string, pulled back as far as he could and let it go.

'Wow! Look at that!'

The arrow soared into the sky, nearly disappeared, and then fell to earth on the far side of the yard, by the tin shed where the electricity generator was housed.

'My turn!' I shouted.

'Only after you've collected the arrow,' Billy said. 'Them arrows are precious. You should always collect 'em right away, otherwise you'll soon have none left. Always meks me laugh in them westerns how they never seem to run out, but them arrows was works of art, lad.'

'Like ours,' I shouted.

Billy chuckled. 'Aye, like ours.'

After I'd fetched the arrow, Billy watched my first attempt, helped me correct my grip, then left me to practise.

'It's been fun, lad, but I can't hang around here all day. I got work to do. Just you be careful wi' that thing, you hear? Put someone's eye out if you're not careful.'

I did hear, but I might as well not have done. I was beside myself with excitement, eager to find Phil and show him what I'd got. But then I had a bright idea. How about if I used my bow and arrow for everybody else's benefit? How about repaying Billy and seeing if I could kill a few of those pigeons he'd been muttering about? Even as the thought unfurled itself in my mind I spotted two plump birds preening themselves on the roof of the farmhouse. Could I get one from here? I picked up four or five of my new arrows and moved slowly towards them. They didn't stir. I moved closer still, until I was sure I was within range. Then I loaded up, took aim and fired one off.

'Nearly,' I muttered, as the arrow slid down the slate roof, clattered against the metal gutter and fell to the ground, disturbing one pigeon, which flew across to the big ash tree and disappeared into the foliage. The other one, meanwhile, had hopped away from the roof, fluttered down and settled right in front of me, on the kitchen window-sill where somebody had left some breadcrusts out for the sparrows. It was a sitting duck, so to speak. I drew the string back as far as it would go, gritted my teeth and drew it back a little more, then let go.

I didn't quite get the pigeon. I almost got it, but of course it moved away as soon as the string went thwunk! My arrow flew through the air, headed straight for the place where the pigeon had been sitting, and through the kitchen window – which was closed. The glass shattered. Bits of it seemed to be flying in every direction. Not that I stayed around to see the full extent of the damage. I grabbed my arrows, slung my bow over my shoulder and ran for the woods.

It seemed as though several hours had passed when I made my way cautiously back towards the farmyard, pausing at the gate. I knew I was starving and had a raging thirst. The car was parked up outside the back entrance, but nobody seemed to be around. I opened the gate and approached the house, straining to see the window, wondering whether my handiwork had been discovered. It had. There was a sheet of plywood over it, and as I stood there, dreading what might happen, out stepped Billy with a hammer in his hand and half a dozen nails between his teeth. Dad was standing next to him. Billy didn't spot me, just went about the business of nailing the plywood firmly in place. I stayed where I was, dreading the moment when Dad would tackle me. But he didn't say a word, just listened to what Billy was telling him.

'Amazing,' he said. 'I watched the bird take off and fly towards the window, and t'next thing was – bits of glass everywhere. You wouldn't think a pigeon could do that, but …'

He tailed off then. He'd seen me out of the corner of his eye, and he half turned and winked at me. I slipped quietly into the barn and put my bow and arrows where nobody would spot them.

A Star is Born

It was a Saturday morning, the first day of the long summer holiday. I was tiptoeing out through the back door with my cricket bat under my arm when I felt a hand on my collar. It was Mum. 'Just a minute, young Michael. Before you go wandering off. I thought I told you to put your sandals on.'

'Girls wear sandals.'

'Very true, Michael. And so do boys, especially in the summertime. If you think I'm going to let you run around all day in your only decent pair of shoes you've another think coming. I want them to last you another term at school.'

'But we're playing cricket. Cricketers wear boots.'

'Which you do not possess.'

I stood there, trying to glower. I'd been watching Just William on the telly and thought he did the best scowl I'd ever seen. 'And it's wet,' I said. 'I might catch pneumonia.'

Mum looked up at the clouds, broken by a stiff breeze and more white than grey. 'Was wet,' she said. 'But the forecast's good. It's sandal weather. End of conversation, you hear?'

I headed for the cupboard where our shoes were kept, and pulled out the dreaded sandals. As it happened, I wasn't heartbroken to take the shoes off. They were too big for me. They always were, when new. The idea was that I'd "grow into them".

'And now ...' Mum began. I wasn't quite sure what was coming, but I knew it would begin with 'seeing as you're going out'. That's why I'd been tiptoeing past her in the first place.

'Seeing as you're going out, there's a few things I need at the shop.'

She had in her hand a piece of cardboard she'd cut from a cereal box. I didn't bother complaining – I knew what the answer would be – but all the same I pulled my 'why is it always me?' face. Had to be worth a try.

'And you can wipe that expression off your face this minute. If you want any tea tonight, you've to pull your weight – the same as everybody else. Goodness knows I've got my hands full with you lot on holiday for six weeks and nothing to do but get into mischief. Now, listen to me. Are you listening?'

She knew I wasn't, and she knew that if by some freak chance I was, I'd still manage to forget whatever it was she wanted me to get. I waited while she wrote her list and handed it over.

'There you are. Six eggs, a packet of lard and a tin of creamed rice. D'you want a basket?'

'A basket?' I said, and pulled my "I'm a boy, remember?" face. The last thing I wanted was for my mates to see me walking down the road with a wicker basket in my hand. I remember how much grief we gave Titch Burton the day he was sent to wheel his baby sister's pram round the park. He never lived that down.

'I don't need a basket,' I said, through gritted teeth.

'Well, don't you go dropping anything – especially those eggs, or you'll be back to the shop to buy some more with your next week's pocket money, d'you hear?'

'Yes, Mum.'

'All right. Here's a pound. And don't forget to stop for the change this time.'

'No, Mum.'

I set off down the Avenue. None of my friends were out yet, but they soon would be. Only the previous day we'd been talking about a cricket game against the Rowan Avenue lot. We were always playing Test matches and footie games against them. Either that or organising pitched battles, generally involving a few brandished sticks, a bit of stone-throwing and a lot of name-calling; or, after the fields were harvested, bombing each other with balls of straw.

I hurried along the snicket and onto the path that led through the churchyard. I stopped on the bridge, leaning over the railings to inspect the slow-moving river. The air was still damp after a thunderstorm the night before; as the wind got up a few odd drips fell from the elder-trees that overhung the far bank. The fish would be rising. One of the boys said he'd caught a pike in there – a big one, he said. But then he could have been exaggerating. Oh well, no time for that just now. I made my way down to the green and the little parade of shops. In the general store I pulled out Mum's list and handed it over the counter, then went and browsed amongst the comics. I pulled out a Beano to catch up on Dennis the Menace's latest escapades. Mum and Dad disapproved of Dennis. They said he set a bad example.

'Now then, do you want this lot or not?'

The shopkeeper was standing there with my purchases, frowning at me. I shoved the comic back into the rack, went to the counter and handed over the pound note Mum had given me. I popped the change in my trouser pocket, stuffed the lard down my shirt and set off for home, carrying the eggs in one hand, the creamed rice in the other. I walked fast, occasionally breaking into a trot. The sun was trying to come out, the grass was drying and surely by now some of the boys would be marking out the pitch. I raced through the churchyard, over the bridge and back along the snicket. I turned into the Avenue and there they were, an upturned cardboard box in place for a wicket, fielders crouched, bowler running in. Tim was batting. He swung at the ball, caught it smack in the middle of his bat and heaved it skyward. I watched, fascinated, as it reached the top of its upward trajectory then started descending.

Martin Longbottom was racing towards me, trying to position himself under the ball and catch it. As he clipped my shoulder he shouted, 'Don't drop your mum's eggs!'

I didn't. Oh no. I clung onto the eggs for dear life. It was the creamed rice I dropped, right on my toe. And it didn't half hurt – especially with no toe-cap to protect me . I picked the tin up, hobbled home and just managed not to start howling till I was inside the back door.

Mum released my grip on the eggs and placed them on the kitchen table.

'Oh dear,' she said, 'what have we done now?'

'The tin – it landed on my toe. And it hurts,' I sniffed. I was about to start crying again when it occurred to me that the whole accident was Mum's fault anyway. 'It wouldn't have happened if you hadn't made me wear them stupid daft sandals,' I spluttered.

'Those stupid daft sandals,' Mum corrected me. 'Not them. Anyway, Michael, you might not have dropped the tinned rice if you hadn't been in such an almighty hurry. Tearing along as usual, I suppose.' It wasn't that Mum was a harsh, insensitive person; just that she'd been here before – many times. She knew all about boys. 'Right,' she sighed, 'let's have a look at it, shall we?'

She squatted down and unbuckled my sandal – and with the pain that caused I couldn't stop myself howling. The strange thing was that for all it hurt there was no obvious sign that anything was wrong, although it was starting to turn red. She prodded the toe carefully with her forefinger. 'Does that hurt?' But I'd already answered her question with a yelp. She tried to move the toe, and I yelped again. She stood up and gave the matter a bit of thought. Then she said, 'Right, young man, I'm afraid it's off to casualty with you.' That stopped me from yelping. I looked up at her.

'Casualty?' I said.

'Yes. It's a trip into York, I'm afraid. We need to get this looked at. In the hospital.'

'Wow!' Suddenly the pain seemed to have eased. 'Are we going to get an ambulance?' I had immediate visions of us racing down Haxby Road, seventy miles an hour, lights flashing and bells ringing and cars swerving out of the way. 'Am I going to sleep in an oxygen tent and have injections and stuff? Like on the telly?' Suddenly life seemed full of exciting possibilities. 'And will the nurses tuck me in at night?' Young as I was I knew that I wanted to marry a nurse when I grew up – so the sooner I got to know one or two the better. There was something about that uniform that already attracted me. And besides, they were trained in looking after people, and there was nothing I liked better than to be looked after.

As I paused for breath, Mum did her best to bring me down to earth. 'I wouldn't get your hopes up, my lad. They'll take an x-ray. See if it's broken. Maybe put a bandage on it.'

'A bandage?' I didn't like the sound of that. If I'd broken something I wanted a pot, like Graham Baker had the time he busted his arm falling out of a tree. He wore that cast for weeks afterwards. Everybody got to write things on it. He even let the girls join in. Some of them put little crosses, and he said they were like promises, and when he took it off they had to kiss him as a sort of payment. Yes, a cast: that's what I needed, and I was about to say so – just so that Mum and everybody else knew exactly where I stood.

But Mum was no longer there. She'd gone to fetch Dad in from the garden, and tell him to get the car out of the garage. He would drive me in and she'd stay home and look after the others who were, she said, not to be trusted alone. I could understand that with Phil, but not the girls. They were just a couple of goody-two-shoes as far as I was concerned. But what did I care about them right now? I was an emergency. I was going to the hospital to have an x-ray taken. With any luck Dad would break the speed limit, and then I'd have a proper operation to re-set my toe, and tonight I'd be tucked into a hospital bed and kissed goodnight by all the nurses. It may not have been high drama to my parents, but in my mind it was up there alongside the circus we went to on the York Knavesmire one time.

Dad didn't break any speed limits, even though I grimaced and winced a lot and said that I hoped it wouldn't take long because I might get gangrene. Looking back, I think he knew what I was after, because he slowed the car down at every grimace, saying he didn't want me to get thrown about as he went round the corners. When we got to casualty we were told to wait. I couldn't understand it. I was an emergency, and here were all these other people who hardly looked ill at all just sitting there reading magazines.

We were there for hours and hours, it seemed to me. And when we finally did get to see someone they started the prodding and pulling all over again and made me yell. Still, that turned out to be a good move on my part, since a pretty young nurse came and stroked my head and told me I'd been a brave boy.

After that came the x-ray – and, as Dad said – actual photographic evidence of my injuries, although as hard as I stared at the murky image I couldn't make out the jagged fracture I'd hope to see.

After that they kept us waiting around for another few hours – although Dad insisted it was no more than twenty minutes – before they let us go home. They hadn't given me the pot I'd been hoping for, but they did let me have a copy of the x-ray photograph. They weren't supposed to, but Dad knew the radiographer and had a word with him. They'd been at school together.

So now I was an invalid. The bad news was that I couldn't play cricket for several days. The good news was that I couldn't be given any household chores. So I was allowed to sit indoors and watch the little bits of daytime telly that were available; or read comics; or play alone in the bedroom – anything, I soon realised, that kept me out of Mum's way while she hurried around doing the cooking and cleaning.

It was during this spell of enforced isolation that I started to watch a TV show that soon became a favourite of mine: Why Don't You …? It was all about things you might do instead of sitting on your backside watching TV. 'Why don't you … why don't you … just switch off your television set and go out and do something less boring instead?' went the theme song. Children would write in and suggest activities, outings, games and so on. It was to play quite a part in my life in the months to come.

There was one other great thing about the accident with the tinned rice pudding. When I was finally allowed out to play once more I was given a brand new pair of trainers Mum had bought to replace the sandals. Not just ordinary trainers, mind you, but Dunlop Green Flash.

'Let's face it,' she said, as she handed them over to me, 'the kind of things you get up to – climbing trees and kicking stones and racing everywhere pell-mell, you need to protect yourself, don't you?'

I was on the point of saying, 'I told you so,' but just as the words were about to escape I saw sense, and shut my mouth.

People say that when they look back it always seems as though summer went on forever, and they never remember being bored as a child. Well, it's parents who come out with that; usually when their kids complain it's … guess what? They're bored. I remember being bored. I remember lying on the grass with nothing better to do than watch the big white and grey clouds go by, and imagining that I was climbing them, right to the very top. I remember being told not to come home until five o'clock because Mum was shampooing the rugs, and checking the clock on top of the school every few minutes, wondering why it took so long to move. Kids do get bored, and time does drag. But the good part of that is that when something unusual comes along the excitement of it is overwhelming.

We were back at school. I remember it was October, because I'd just got into trouble for bruising Trevor Bellingham's hand with my conker. It was his fault. He moved just when I was taking aim at his. I caught him right across the knuckles, and he started swelling up immediately. Then of course he started blubbering and I was the one who got sent to the headmistress.

It wasn't the first time I'd been up to her study. The previous occasion was when I was caught climbing over the wall and scrabbling up the coke-pile – which was strictly out of bounds. That wasn't my fault either. We were playing football and Danny Bridges had kicked the ball way up in the air, where the wind had carried it into the mound of fuel. Okay, I was the one who volunteered to go after it, but his job was to stand look-out, in case one of the teachers came by – and he got so interested, watching me climb three steps up and slide two steps back, that he didn't notice Mr Adams approaching. I got a couple of whacks on my backside for that – and lost two weeks' pocket money when I got home and Mum found the rip in my trousers where I'd skidded down the mound clutching the ball. To make matters worse, Mr Adams confiscated the ball for a week.

Anyway, the point of all this is that it was definitely conker-time when the news broke. It was announced in assembly that the BBC had written to the school asking if they could address us. It seemed that the producers of that programme I'd been watching, Why Don't You ...?, wanted to know if any of us had any unusual or interesting hobbies. If we did, we might feature on the show. Now this really did exercise my mind. The idea of being on the telly – well, that was strictly for famous people, wasn't it? How often would an ordinary person from a Yorkshire village get on? And a child at that? I knew right away that I had to be that child. Which meant that I had to come up with a strange or exotic hobby. Soon.

I thought about the problem. I thought about it long and hard. And the more I thought the more worried I became. The fact was, I didn't have a hobby at all. I was too busy having fun to settle down and get absorbed in something the way other kids did. Too inquisitive: always wandering off in the fields or hanging around farmyards watching the animals and machinery. I was too impatient as well. I'd tried stamp collecting but couldn't be bothered with trying to lick all those tiny paper hinges that kept them in the album. Somehow all the pages ended up getting stuck together, and when I forced them apart the stamps got ripped. I tried Meccano, but made the mistake of trying to build a crane outside. When I dropped all the nuts and bolts I could only watch as half of them rolled down the drain at the side of the house. I tried bird-watching one time when Phil and I spotted a kingfisher down by the beck. I even persuaded Dad to lend me his binoculars, but it seemed that we only ever saw sparrows, rooks and the odd blackbird. Half an hour of that and I was bored to death. And half frozen.

So, when the big day arrived and the BBC were due to show up, I set off for school without the faintest idea as to what I was going to say. I knew I had to say something, because I had promised myself that I was going to be on that show, no matter what. Inspiration came quite unexpectedly. It came as I walked down our road. The idea was so brilliant that I could barely keep it to myself as I entered through the school gate and waited for the whistle that would see us line up and troop into assembly.

Mostly we thought of assembly as the boring bit before we got to the even more boring bit: lessons, which in those days always seemed to start off with arithmetic. This day, however, I was all ears. When the big moment came, when we were asked to put up our hands and tell the guest from the BBC about our unusual hobby, I was on my feet, jumping up and down.

'Yes,' said the headmistress. 'Is that Michael Pannett over there with his hand in the air?'

'Yes, miss.'

'And tell us, what is your hobby, Michael?'

I took a deep breath, paused and looked around me. I wanted to make quite sure that everybody was listening. This was going to be a big moment. 'My hobby ...' I began. It seemed that everybody in the hall was staring at me – including Tim, who was going to play a vital role in this scheme. 'My hobby,' I continued, 'is ... is ...'

'Well, carry on, Michael, do tell us.'

'Making weathervanes!' I blurted it out and sat down.

There was a moment's silence, followed by a scattering of laughter. Then the headmistress said, 'Well. What an extraordinary thing to do, Michael. And you've kept it secret from us all this time. Why is that?'

Talk about thinking on your feet. There was our headmistress giving me the hard stare, and there was my friend Tim, whose collection of home-made weathervanes I'd been looking at that very morning, his eyes all but popping out of his head. Everybody else seemed to be stifling giggles.

'Well,' I began, 'it's an unusual sort of hobby and I just – I just thought people would laugh at me. That's why I never said anything.'

The headmistress was trying to speak, but nobody could hear a word she was saying. The place was in uproar. When she finally got everybody calmed down I heard her say, 'Well, I'm sure we'll all look forward to hearing more about these weathervanes. Maybe you can tell everybody a bit about them. Do stand up, Michael and address us all.'

I gulped, rose to my feet once more and said, 'Well, weathervanes are really interesting. They have cockerels and things, and they go around.' Everybody had turned around to stare at me, blank looks in their eyes. They seemed to want more. I coughed and carried on. 'Yes, they go round and round and tell you where the wind's coming from, and that way you know when it's going to rain.' Still they stared. 'And you get 'em on church steeples and that.' I glanced down and saw Tim looking up at me. He was either awestruck or speechless with anger because I was stealing his hobby. I wasn't sure. 'And some people,' I said, 'some people keep them in their garden to scare cats away. But I keep mine in – in my bedroom.'

I dried up then. I wasn't bad at making stuff up in those days, and I generally had something to say for myself, but I was running out of ideas. I looked at the headmistress who smiled and said,

'Very good, Michael. You may sit down now.'

Lots of other kids now put up their hands and told the headmistress about their hobbies – and most of them were telling the truth, as far as I could tell. It was an uncomfortable feeling, realising what I might have got myself into. Tim, of course, was the first to grab me as we trooped out of the hall and into our classroom.

'Who are you trying to kid?' he said. 'You don't make weathervanes. I do. Well, me Dad does.'

'So why didn't you put your hand up?' I said. 'Listen, you want to be on telly, don't you?'

'Well, yeah. I wouldn't mind.'

'Right, so we'll do it together. We might get discovered and – you know, be famous, both of us.'

'Yes but …'

'But what?'

'But they're not my weathervanes to play about with. They're me Dad's. Didn't you hear what I said?'

'That's all right,' I said. 'We only need to borrow them – for a day or two. How long do you think they'll be around, the BBC?'

'Search me.'

This was all very exciting, but for a little while I managed to forget about the BBC. Conker season was coming to an end, but that meant we were into autumn, and autumn meant one thing: fireworks.

The Fifth of November was still several weeks away, but down at the end of the Avenue, on a patch of waste ground, we'd already started to gather the materials for our neighbourhood bonfire.

When I say neighbourhood, I mean our street. Park Avenue was a cul de sac. There was no through traffic; there were fields to either side and there was Joseph Rowntree secondary school at the top end; Rowan Avenue, home of our arch-enemies, was across the field. We were isolated, protected, safe. And the waste ground, the rough grassy area we played on, and built our annual bonfire on, was our own little wilderness.

As September gave way to October and the leaves started to turn yellow and fall to the ground in the gales that blew in from the west, we started looking for fallen branches to drag down to the middle of the field. We salvaged any waste timber that we found. If somebody was throwing out any old furniture, we grabbed that too, and by the time October turned into November, we had a fine big mound of combustible material awaiting a guy to sit on the top.

'It's gonna be the size of Mount Everest,' we told ourselves.

But the bonfire, and the rising excitement as Guy Fawkes drew nearer, couldn't entirely dispel the nagging worry at the back of my mind, the fact that I'd dug myself a great big hole with this weathervane caper. A week or two after I'd made my bid for stardom two BBC researchers visited the school – or so we were told in assembly.

'What you going to do?' Tim asked me one damp, foggy morning as we dragged an old wooden pallet down to the bonfire site. 'Have you told your Mum and Dad yet?'

'I don't dare.'

Tim could see it from my point of view. And now that he'd had time to think about it he desperately wanted to be on TV too. 'Tell you what,' he said, 'why don't I tell my Dad that we're doing it together?'

'How do you mean?'

Tim thought for a moment, then said, 'Well, I'll tell him it was your idea.'

'What, and I asked you if I could – ?'

'Yeah, borrow them.'

Well, that was the plan, but before we had a chance to put it into action, fate intervened – or so it seemed.

I was at home. I can't remember what I was doing, but I took little notice when the phone rang. Why would I? The only time I picked up the phone was when nobody was around to see me – and that wasn't to make a call. Very few of my friends had phones back then, and even if we'd bothered to write down each other's numbers, what would we say? Ours was a party line. It was cheaper that way. One of our favourite pastimes was picking it up to see whether we could eavesdrop on our neighbours' conversations – and then cough or groan, or breathe heavily. Well, we were young …

'It's for you.' Mum was standing over me, holding the phone.

'You what?'

'You mean pardon.' She thrust the receiver towards me. 'It's the BBC. They want to talk to you.' She narrowed her eyes. 'If you've been up to something you'll have me and your father to answer to.'

People speak of going hot and cold all over. Trust me, it happens. It was indeed the BBC. They had decided that mine was the most interesting hobby of all the ones they'd heard about at school, and they wanted to come and visit me and have a look at the weathervanes.

I now had some explaining to do. I started with Mum but she folded her arms and stopped me. It was a classic case of 'Wait till your father gets home'.

Dad arrived home at a quarter to six, as usual, and Mum was at the front window waiting for him to ride up on his moped. She had the back door open as he came in from the garage. Phil, Gillian and Christine were all clustered around the kitchen door. They knew trouble was brewing and they wanted a ringside seat.

'Hello, Jeff dear.' Mum gave him the usual kiss on the cheek, then said, 'You may as well find out now as later. I've just discovered that our youngest son here has a secret talent.' She turned to me. 'Now, are you going to tell him, or shall I?' I didn't answer. I managed a strangled sort of gulp, but couldn't force any words out. 'Well,' she said, 'it seems that Michael is an expert in weathervane construction.'

She told the tale, and I enlarged upon it. Then she added a bit more. Dad took it all in, told me I'd done a very stupid thing, and said, 'Right. The first nothing is for you to go around to your friend's house and explain to his mother and father what you've done.' He looked at Mum. 'I think we should do that now, before tea, don't you?'

She agreed. We went and knocked on Tim's door. His dad answered.

'Ah, Mister Rigg,' Dad said. 'Sorry to bother you at this time but Michael here has something to tell you.'

Who'd be a grown-up? After I'd confessed to Mister Rigg, and listened as he told me that I'd been a very silly boy, a very naughty boy, and that this was going to cause him a lot of bother, he calmed down. Just for a moment. Then he got all wound up again and said, 'Apart from anything, your thoughtless actions are going to make me look very silly. I only have five or six weathervanes out there. They'll be expecting dozens.' He put his hand to his head and said, 'Look, why don't you come inside and we'll think this through.'

We sat down with Tim, his mum and dad, and the grown-ups talked over the best way to handle the thing.

'We can't stall the BBC,' Mister Rigg said.

Dad agreed. 'No, we can't do that. It'd hardly be fair on them, would it?'

They both thought for a minute, then Tim's mum said, 'How about joining forces – and putting on a real show for them?'

Tim's dad brightened. 'You mean – what, make a few more?'

'Why not? They didn't take you long, and with three of us' – she looked enquiringly at Dad, who nodded – 'well, surely we could manage.'

Mister Rigg was brightening by the minute. 'All right,' he said, and turned to Dad. 'How about if we move the existing vanes into your garden, then put in a solid weekend's work? Pull out all the stops.'

'All hands to the pump,' Dad added.

And so it was agreed. We would pull the wool over the BBC's eyes, we would muck in – and I would be off the hook. As to producing the extra vanes, that was for Dad and Mister Rigg. Tim and I were given the job of ferrying cups of tea to them as they hammered and sawed – the occasional Elastoplast too – and were then given the paints and brushes and left to get on with it. While we did that, the two dads assembled a fresh set of parts and gave us careful instructions so that we could assemble one for the cameras – and the millions of viewers.

Two weeks later the BBC crew showed up: cameraman, sound man, long-haired director, a woman with a clipboard and one or two other people. Impressed? We were awestruck. As were our neighbours, who crowded around the front gate ooh-ing and aah-ing. We did as instructed, answered a few questions about our amazing hobby and then, as suddenly as they'd arrived, the crew were on their way.

But that wasn't the end of the excitement. Far from it. A few weeks later we got word that we were to be featured on the Saturday morning programme. We all gathered round the TV to watch – me and Phil, Mum and Dad, the girls, Petra, and of course our Aunt June who was paying us her fortnightly visit.

That was the only downside of the whole weekend. Aunt June, delightful as she was, had somehow persuaded Mum and Dad that she could cut hair. And so she attacked me with her scissors, leaving me with very little hair – and what there was sticking up at all angles.

After the excitement of the TV show, Tim and I couldn't wait to get to school on Monday. We knew what to expect, and even spent Sunday afternoon practising our autographs. We weren't disappointed. This was my first taste of celebrity, and I couldn't get enough. We were mobbed. We were indeed asked to sign exercise books, autograph books, one or two plaster casts and several forearms. So now I had my sights on a new career. Never mind being a train driver, a caterpillar driver, a demolition man. I now decided I would be a TV star.

Butter Wouldn't Melt

Some of the biggest rogues you'll ever meet in life started out as choirboys. It's a well known fact. To be fair, the same goes for vicars' sons – and a few of their daughters, I would later discover; but this is about choirboys. Those sweet little choristers learn at an early age that they're special, a breed apart. They know when they appear, with their white ruffs around their necks and their hymnbooks in their hands, that all eyes are on them. And they soon learn that in the view of the congregation they're second cousins to the angels they sing about. Butter wouldn't melt in their mouths. What the congregation tend to forget is, they're boys. And we all know what boys are. The fact is, choirboys get away with murder – and they expect to carry on getting away with it for the rest of their lives. I know. I was one of those angelic little fellows. Once upon a time.

It's all about appearances. It's all a pretence. It starts in the vestry when those fresh-faced, freshly scrubbed boys spit out their chewing-gum – peppermint flavoured in some cases, to hide the smell of the cigarettes – put on their most pious expressions, shove their comics down the back of their trousers, straighten their ruffs and smocks, and troop into the church. The congregation watch as they take their seats in the ornately carved choir-stalls and wait for the signal from the choirmaster, or the organist. They listen, enraptured, as a chorus of angelic voices soars into the timbered roof, and, in the case of the women, their hearts melt. Oh, look at the little darlings. Aren't they sweet?

Sweet? When I followed my mate Kev into the choir at the Parish Church of All Saints and Saint Andrew, there was only one thing on my mind.

'Money,' said Kev. 'It's all about the money.'

We were standing by the lych-gate on a Sunday morning, kicking at the drifts of pink and white confetti that had gathered under the arched entrance after a wedding that had taken place the previous day. Kev was on his way to morning service. I was at a loose end. I couldn't go home or they'd rope me in to help with the housework, so that was why I'd walked down to the church with him. Kev's remark puzzled me. We didn't go a lot. My parents weren't very religious. We went about once a month, and of course Christmas, Easter and Mothering Sunday. So I was quite familiar with the order of service, as I was with the collection plate – in our case a big, inlaid brass platter which I'd watched, fascinated, as it was passed from hand to hand, all laden with copper and silver coins. Was that what Kev meant when he said it was all about money?

'Do you mean you get paid?' I asked him.

'Paid? I should say so.' He dug into his trousers and pulled out a handful of coins, mostly silver. 'Got this yesterday. Five bob,' he said. 'Twenty-five pence in new money. That's for a wedding. We get loads of them, this time of year. And christenings.' He shrugged and dropped the coins back in his pocket. 'Funerals too. And then some folk, if you give 'em a smile, you'll get a tip. Not at funerals, like, but weddings … aye, I got a ten-bob note one time.'

'Wow. But what about normal Sundays?' I asked. 'Like today.'

'No,' he said. 'Normal Sundays you don't get paid. But, it's like the vicar said in his sermon the other week, you take the rough with the smooth.' He paused, hooked his thumbs over his new leather belt and leaned back on his heels. 'Course, Sundays – if you're lucky … See, today's Communion – so you might get … well, you know.' He made a sort of twisting motion with his hand to his mouth, and winked.

'Ah,' I said. 'Right.' I hadn't a clue what he was on about, but I nodded my head all the same. Kev was always a step ahead of the rest of us. He had a big brother, Steve, a real tough guy, and he got to know all sorts of things he shouldn't have known at his age. Steve had a girlfriend. He had been in pubs. There was a rumour that he'd been on probation too. No wonder we all looked up to him.

'Yeah, if you're really crafty,' Kev said, smacking his lips and winking at me, 'you can get a drink of the holy wine.' He jingled the coins in his pocket. 'So long as the vicar doesn't cop you, of course. But the money's the thing.' He looked at his watch, a shiny thing with a dark blue face and a black plastic wristband. 'See this?' he said. 'I saved up for that in six weeks. It glows in the dark.'

'Wow.'

'And the belt. Good, isn't it?'

I had to admit it was a very fine belt, the sort of thing a cowboy might wear.

Just then a car came up the lane. 'I'd better get going,' Kev said. 'That's old Mitchell, the choirmaster.' Before I could respond he added, 'Can't be late or there's big trouble.' Then, as he turned to go he said, 'You ought to come and watch us. Maybe see if you can get an audition. They're always looking for new choirboys. It's the big lads, see. Their voices break and ...' He drew a finger theatrically across his throat. 'That's them done for. Here one day, gone the next. They have to go and get a paper-round. Have to work for their money.' He laughed, and said, 'Okay, see you, Mike.'

Kev was off at a gallop. I stood and watched him dash through the cemetery. Pretty soon the congregation started to arrive and I got out from under the lych-gate. I went and stood by the war memorial. There were still a couple of poppy wreaths laid at the base of it. It made me think about Grandpa, who was in the First World War but never spoke about it. I wondered whether he knew any of the names carved on the stone. Maybe I'd ask him some time.

I watched the congregation walking by. I thought about what Kev had said. Then I remembered the carol concert we'd had at school the previous Christmas and how I'd been told to stand at the front and sing as loud as I could, because I was one of the best singers in class. 'He can certainly hold a tune, that boy of yours,' my teacher told Mum one day when she bumped into her in town. And Mum told the whole family at tea that night. Yes, I enjoyed a good sing-song. Didn't mind some of the hymns we did in assembly either. But joining the choir? No thankyou. But of course, I hadn't had the conversation with Kev yet. That changed everything.

I waited until everybody had gone into the church, then walked slowly along the path, pausing to read some of the headstones. There was one that always fascinated me. It stood against the old brick wall that marked the boundary of the churchyard. It said, 'In a small vault near here are deposited the ashes of the late Charlotte Elizabeth Richardson, died 13th December 1889'. I looked at the bare, dusty ground. The idea that people – actual dead people – were under my feet sort of thrilled me and frightened me in equal measure.

I approached the main entrance to the church, pushed at the big wooden door and opened it a few inches. They were singing a hymn, one I knew well. 'Hills of the North Rejoice'. I could see the choir, right at the top end of the church, all dressed in red and looking – well, to tell the truth I'd always thought they looked a right bunch of sissies. But then I thought of the money, and Kevin. And his big brother. He'd been in the choir too, and he was no sissy. Neither was Kev. I remembered the time Kev borrowed his brother's airgun and shot a wood pigeon. I was about to step inside when an old woman with white hair and liver-spots on the back of her hand appeared noiselessly from the shadows and tried to give me a hymn-book. She smelled of lavender, like Aunt Annie at Staintondale. But, seeing this old lady's wrinkled neck and hooked nose, all I could think of was Charlotte Elizabeth Richardson. I shrank away from her, let the door swing and ran back across the cemetery as fast as my legs would carry me.

It didn't put me off, though. Where money was concerned I was always interested. I'd got to that age when I wanted as much money as I could get. There were toys I wanted to buy, and sweets, and comics and such things, and my pocket money never seemed to last beyond Saturday afternoon. The following Wednesday, after tea, I met up with Kev and walked down the narrow path that cut through to the river Foss, beyond which was the churchyard.

'You sure it's okay?' I asked him, as we crossed the bridge.

'Yeah, I told him you'd be coming.'

'What'll I have to do?'

'Practise. That's what it's called. Choir practice.'

'Yeah but … what about me? How will he know I'm good enough.'

'Oh, you know – he'll get you to sing something for him.'

'Like what?'

'Whatever he says. Might be a hymn, might be a psalm. Might be one o' them Latin things. From the Prayer Book, like.'

'Latin? I don't know any Latin.'

Kev laughed. 'You don't have to. I never know what they're on about. We just sing what's on the page and everybody's happy.' He slapped me in the stomach with the back of his hand. 'Don't worry, it's all written down. And he'll play it through on the piano, or maybe he'll fire up the organ – and he always sings through everything himself before we have a go.' He put his hand in his pocket. 'Here, have a Fishermen's Friend. Clear your throat for you.'

I needn't have worried. Mister Mitchell, the choirmaster, was a decent sort of fellow. He took me into the vestry, where all the vicar's clothes were hung up, and the choirboys' smocks, and got me to sing to him, solo and unaccompanied. It was 'The Lord's My Shepherd', and I knew that all right – from school. Then he took me into the church itself – the nave, as he called it – where I sang along with the other lads. An hour later, after we'd gone through three or four hymns and one of those Latin jobs, I was in. Practice every Wednesday night, and you had to be at church twice on a Sunday. Weddings and so on as required.

Before I left that night, Mister Mitchell gave me my smock and a pair of white ruffs.

'It may not fit,' he said, 'but I dare say you'll grow into it. Or you may prevail upon your mother to alter it for you. It's up to you to keep it clean, of course. I don't like my boys looking scruffy, understand?'

Mum did as requested, but it still felt weird, wearing what looked to me suspiciously like a girl's dress. To save time I threw it on over my shirt before I pedalled down to church every Wednesday and Sunday (and weddings on a Saturday, as required) but I made sure I tucked it in like a shirt. Apart from hiding my embarrassment, it made sure it didn't get covered in grease off my chain.

I'll never forget my first performance. It was a Sunday, morning service. The first hymn was an old favourite, 'For Those In Peril On The Sea', one I was more than familiar with. I'd even heard Phil sing it around the house. Desperate to make an impression, I took a deep breath, threw out my chest and gave it my all. I was halfway through the second verse when I glanced up at Mister Mitchell, hoping he would approve. He didn't. I got what would become the familiar 'stare', meaning 'cut it out or you're in trouble'.

I had several good years as a chorister. I made some great tips at weddings, and once got to sing at a special service in York Minster. They paid us all a pound for that, and as I made my way home from there I couldn't imagine how life could get any better.

Gunpowder, Treason & Plot

'Go on, outside with you. I can't have you cluttering the place up all morning.'

Mum was spring-cleaning – or so she said. Pointing out to her that this was November and I was on my half-term holiday didn't cut much ice at all. She was on a mission. The girls were playing at their friends' house, Phil had gone to York on the bus, and as for me, I was simply in the way.

'But it's cold out there,' I whined.

'Outside,' she repeated, thrusting a dripping mop to within an inch of my face. 'Unless you want to get a bucket and start scrubbing that floor. I've a whole list of jobs. There's cupboard doors to wash, shelves to clean out, that glory-hole under the stairs, all that rubbish under your bed … you can take your pick.'

When it came to getting us out of the house, and fast, Mum held all the aces. I grabbed my coat, shoved my York City hat on my head, ran out the back door and made my way onto the street. I looked up and down. There wasn't a soul to be seen. Why would there be, on a day like this? I trudged off down the Avenue, shoulders hunched, hands in pockets. With a whole morning stretching in front of me I tried to cheer myself up whistling a tune I'd heard on the radio. But every time I pursed my lips the wind took my breath away. It was one of those nasty, unruly autumn days with sudden blasts of cold air and spots of icy rain. I plodded on, head down. I was bored. I was cold. I was fed up. And there seemed to be nobody to play with.

I'd gone about fifty yards when I heard a sort of scraping, rustling noise. Looking up, I saw a tree about fifty yards ahead of me – or half a tree, at any rate. It was a beech, its grey branches covered in golden brown leaves. It seemed to be propelling itself down the middle of the road, along the white line. Wow, I thought, this must be quite a wind blowing. Then I realised that the tree was going against the wind. This was weird. I broke into a run, and caught up with it. As I did so, it came to a standstill.

'Oh hello, Mike. Give us a hand, will you?'

As his head popped up from amongst the foliage I saw it was my mate Alan, leaning forward with a branch across his chest, his face red and his nose running.

'Where we off?' I asked, ducking underneath and grabbing a branch of my own.

He panted a couple of times then said, 'To t'bonfire, of course. Where else?'

'Oh. Right.'

There was never any real organisation behind the annual Avenue bonfire, no planning, no notices outside the post office, no admission fee, no designated adult setting off the fireworks, no food stalls. Everybody just did their own thing, chipped in, and it always seemed to work. Especially the building of it.

We marched on down the road, in step, dragging the tree behind us.

'Where'd you get this then?' I asked, as we approached the entrance to the field and paused for a breather.

Alan looked around as if he was about to share some great secret. He needn't have bothered. The street was still deserted. Everybody was indoors, it seemed – where any sane person would be on a day like this.

'I found it,' he said. 'Well, it was in someone's garden but it was – you know, sort of hanging over the path. Public property, so I gave it a pull and away it came. Brought half the fence down with it,' he added, then laughed. 'They'll blame the wind, won't they?'

A full gale was now sweeping all before it – fallen leaves, one of last night's fish-and-chip wrappers, a stray hub-cap rattling down the gutter and one forlorn looking crow hopping along trying to maintain its balance. I agreed that the tree's owner would indeed blame the elements. We trudged on and barged through the entrance to the field, manhandling the branch over the gate, before stopping again to get our breath. I was feeling better now. I had company, I had a purpose, and I'd warmed myself up. Suddenly it felt the way a half-term holiday should.

Autumn was a great time for us kids. Each year, once we'd got used to being back at school and broken our new teacher in, we enjoyed everything that autumn had to offer.

First would come those wonderful Saturday mornings when word would get out that someone had found a tree laden with plump, shiny conkers. We'd set off from all corners, a whole gang of us armed with the biggest, stoutest sticks we could find, converging on the designated tree. Once there we'd hurl our cudgels, as we liked to call them, into the branches to dislodge the spiky green fruit. When we'd stripped the tree bare, stuffed our pockets, and dropped any extra conkers down our jumpers, we'd take them home and see whether we could persuade our mothers to pop them in the oven, or put them in vinegar overnight. That toughened them beautifully. We knew it was cheating. But we also knew that everybody was at it. You rarely started a conker game without the ritual sniffing of each other's weapons, and muttered accusations about ovens and pickling. But only an idiot went into battle with an untreated conker. Replace that and it was lambs to the slaughter.

Once the conker season passed, of course, we only had one thing on our mind. It was the most exciting time of the year apart from Christmas. Guy Fawkes, November the fifth. Gunpowder, treason and plot – not that we bothered too much with the history side of it. This was just the best excuse anybody ever dreamed up for having a huge fire and a lot of explosions. It was what we boys longed for. I remember sitting in school one day, gazing at the calendar, counting the days and wondering how grown-ups maintained any interest in life without being able to look forward to firework night.

But then grown-ups were a total mystery to me. It seemed to me that their lives were very, very dull. Nothing but work and worry. I had no desire to be one, ever. Why should I? Anyway, that was all years in the future, so far off in fact that I couldn't imagine it. I chose to believe that it would never happen. Life was too good as it was. Why wish it different?

To add to the sense of anticipation as November approached, week by week we watched the waste timber, cast-off furniture and unwanted shrubs pile up in the middle of the field and imagined the great day when it would go up in flames.

Sometimes there'd be a carpet, or a bale of straw. Once there was an old suitcase full of mildewed books. Another time someone put a couple of car tyres in there, and we all speculated as to how they'd burn. Smokily, was the answer.

And who could forget the time Phil shoved an old aerosol can in there? Nearly blew the thing to the four corners of the field. There was hell to pay for that, especially for me: I was the one who grassed him up to Mum and Dad. Under pressure, of course.

Along with the anticipation, however, there was always a nagging worry. What if someone decided to put a match to our precious fire? We'd heard stories at school, and had warnings in assembly. Every so often we'd see smoke from way across the fields as somebody's bonfire was prematurely ignited. All it took was one bad lad – and there were quite a few of those around – and a single match. I could see the temptation right enough.

And so we kept watch – we as a community, I mean. We didn't mount guard, exactly, but the dog-owners in the street amended their late-night walks to take in a circuit of the field, and we kids checked it almost daily. Every time it rained you'd be sure to hear some grown-up say, 'Oh well, at least the bonfire'll be safe for another day or two.'

As we approached the big day, the tension mounted. But before

Guy Fawkes actually arrived we had another treat to look forward to. The fourth of November is special in Yorkshire. It's known as Mischief Night, or Mischievous Night. Traditionally it's the one time of the year when children can commit minor acts of vandalism, and grown-ups, for once, are supposed to see the funny side of it – just providing that nobody goes too far.

For us, acceptable misdemeanours could include anything that came under the heading of 'harmless fun'. What that meant was you could do the kinds of things your parents would admit to having done 'when we were your age' – things like tying someone's door-knocker to their neighbour's, throwing a water-bomb at their windows; swapping garden gates around or smearing black grease on their doorknobs – but of course, there were always people who would get carried away and do the things that our parents also did, but wouldn't admit to: setting fire to somebody's dustbin – metal ones in those days, not plastic – or breaking the odd outhouse window; or, the thing we all dreaded, putting that fateful match to the communal bonfire.

Alan and I dragged our half tree across the grass, propped it against the stack of rubbish and stood back to admire what was the biggest bonfire we'd yet seen. 'Blimey,' Alan said, 'it's bigger than our house, that is.'

'Yeah,' I said, 'and there's still tomorrow. It's gonna get even bigger.'

'My Dad's bringing our old wardrobe down.'

'A wardrobe? Wow.'

'It's got woodworm. It won't half burn. It's got all veneer on it. It's gonna be fantastic,' he said. 'Hey, have your mum and dad got your fireworks yet?'

''Spect so,' I said. 'But they always hide them.'

'Same here,' he said. 'Anyway, what about tonight? Mischief Night. What we going to do?'

I picked up an old wooden pallet that had fallen off the fire, and tried to throw it to the top. 'Dunno. Water-bombs? Ringing doorbells?' The pallet fell back down.

'Nah, I did that last year.' He thought for a moment, bent down to give me a hand and between us we got the pallet halfway up the pile, where it rocked gently in the wind. Then he said, 'Tell you what, let's get Tim and Martin. Make up a gang.'

'Good idea.'

'Here, you got any money?'

'A bit.' I dipped a hand into my pocket and pulled out a five-pence piece and a few coppers.

Alan dug deep. 'I got ten pence here.' He had another dig. 'Make it twelve,' he said. 'Reckon we got enough to buy some eggs?'

'I dunno. How much do they cost?'

'No idea.'

'Anyway, what do we want eggs for?'

'For tonight, of course.'

'I don't get it.'

Alan laughed. 'Don't you know anything? We throw 'em at folks' doors. My Dad said that's what they did when he was little. Takes ages to clean it off. Right laugh.'

'Aye,' I said. 'Aye, that'd be great.' I wasn't convinced, but I didn't want to sound chicken. 'But what if we can't afford 'em?'

Alan kicked at the beech tree. 'Have to think of something else then.'

'Tell you what,' I said, 'we've always got loads of eggs in the pantry. Mum brings a tray home every week. There's thirty. We'll go to my place and – you know, borrow a few.'

'How d'you mean, borrow?'

'We-ell ...'

'You mean nick.'

He was right. Always called a spade a spade, did Alan. And it made me feel a bit uncomfortable.

'Tell you what,' I said, 'How about we all bring a few, then they won't notice.'

'You're on. You get Tim and I'll get Martin. We'll have a ton of eggs.'

'Brilliant.'

'Meet up after tea then. Okay?'

'Okay.'

I'd been on a couple of Mischief Night forays in previous years, both times with Phil and a couple of his mates. The first year we tied toilet rolls to Petra's tail and sent her haring around the neighbourhood in pursuit of a chocolate-flavoured ball. She decorated the Avenue in grand style, trailing toilet tissue up and down garden paths, round gates and lamp-posts. The following year we went out with a tube of toothpaste, the one with the red stripes in it, and spread dollops of it on all our neighbours' front door-knobs, then on a couple of car mirrors and a bicycle saddle. We got away with it too – despite the fact that ours was just about the only house that wasn't hit, a fact that Dad pointed out at teatime next day. I remember there was a long silence after he announced the mysterious outbreak, but somehow Phil and I kept a straight face. This plan, however – going out armed with eggs – seemed much more daring, kind of grown-up.

That evening I waited until we'd finished our tea, then asked if I could go over to Alan's house.

'Oh yes, and what are you going to get up to round there?' Mum asked. I had an answer ready for her.

'He's got these books,' I said. 'On dinosaurs and that.'

It was a lie, of course, but it was a good lie. Mum and Dad liked the idea of me associating with scholarly boys.

'Dinosaurs, eh? Well, all right then,' Mum said, 'but I don't want you late back, even if it is half-term.'

Dad looked at me over the top of his Evening Press. 'And just because it's November the fourth,' he said, 'that doesn't mean you have a licence to create mayhem around the neighbourhood, you hear? We had enough of that last year.'

'Oh, is it the fourth already?' I said, and just to add a little lustre to the pretence I rubbed my hands and said, 'Wow, so that means

November the fifth tomorrow. I can't wait.' All this time, of course, I was wondering how I was going to get into the pantry unobserved. Then I had a brainwave. It's remarkable how solutions present themselves to you out of thin air, just when you need them. I waited till everyone had finished eating, cleared my throat and said, 'Er, shall I wash the pots tonight? Must be my turn by now.'

There was a short silence. Then Phil blew his nose, loudly. Christine and Gillian both looked at me, their mouths hanging open. Dad rustled his paper. Mum frowned and put on her concerned look.

'D'you want me to take your temperature?' she said. 'You're not feverish, are you?'

They all thought that was dead funny. Even I laughed.

'No,' I said, 'just thought I'd be helpful. Like you're always telling me.'

'And seeing that we're letting you go out to your friend's house,' Mum said. I thought there would be more, but she let it go at that. She got up from the table and said, 'Well, come along everybody. We don't want to get in your brother's way, do we?' And out they trooped, all except Phil who lingered a moment, pretending to do his shoelace up.

He waited until he was sure everybody was out of earshot. 'Okay, what's going on?' he asked.

I put the plug in the sink and turned on the hot tap. 'Nothing. Just being helpful, like I said. I've decided to turn over a new leaf.'

'You? A new leaf? Give over.'

'No, honest. It was in the sermon on Sunday, about helping other people. It's worth it in the end. When you die you go to Heaven.'

'Yeah, as if you ever listen to the sermon. I bet you had your head buried in a comic.'

He stared at me, and I stared back. I was sure my face was going red, but I was determined not to let him in on my secret.

'Listen,' he said, pointing his finger at me, 'I was in the choir, remember? I know what goes on.' He narrowed his eyes and gave me the hard stare. 'Don't you worry, matey,' he said. 'I'll find out, and if it's some sort of Mischief Night thing, who knows, I might just decide to blackmail you.'

I didn't answer. I poured the washing-up liquid into the sink and watched the bubbles form. I knew I had nothing to worry about. He'd be at his girlfriend's house all evening. As he turned to go I scooped up a dollop of suds and flicked it at his back. It landed right between his shoulders and stuck there, wobbling like a jelly as he left the room. That'd show him.

I hurried through the dishes, emptied the sink, then tiptoed out into the hallway. They were all in the front room with the telly on. Tomorrow's World. They'd be there for the next hour, all except Dad. He loved this programme, but the minute it was over he would be leaving the room. He never stayed around for Top of The Pops. Mum did sometimes, but not Dad. He didn't reckon much to pop music.

Back in the kitchen, I opened the pantry door. There was the egg-tray, almost full. There must have been a couple of dozen, some smeared with blood or dirt, one or two with feathers sticking to them. I picked out a couple and looked around for a bag but couldn't find one. Instead I put them down inside my sweater. The question on my mind now was, how many did I dare take? I took two more and placed those carefully with the first pair. Suddenly there seemed to be an awful lot of empty spaces in the tray. Could I take a couple more? I hesitated, then thought better of it. I slipped out, closed the pantry door, then went quietly into the hallway and collected my coat.

'Bye!' I shouted. No answer. I could see through the half-open door that they were all glued to the telly. I stood for a moment with my nose pressed against the crack in the door. William Woollard was holding what looked like a shiny plastic round thing. He said it was a compact disc and it was going to revolutionise music. Wouldn't scratch, didn't need a needle. I could hear Dad saying, 'That's the future for you, girls. Remarkable.'

Outside the wind had dropped, the sky had cleared and frost was sparkling on the pavement. I hurried down to our rendezvous, at the gate that led into the field. Alan was there, shoulders hunched inside his big brother's parka. It was about three sizes too big and looked more like a tent.

'Got 'em?' he asked.

'Yeah,' I said, and was about to pat my stomach before I thought better of it. 'Down me sweater here. Four.'

'That all?'

'They're big 'uns,' I said. 'Size of duck's eggs. Anyway, what have you got?'

Alan unzipped the parka and brought out a long grey egg-box. 'Dozen,' he said. 'Once the others show up we're off, right?'

They weren't long. And between them they had another dozen.

'Armed to the teeth,' said Martin. 'Let's go, shall we?'

'Okay then.'

'Where?' Tim said. 'Where we gonna start?'

Alan pointed to the large house right across from where we were standing. 'How about that one there?'

We walked to the front gate. There was a gravelled drive about twenty yards long, leading to the front door. A light was shining in the porch. Otherwise the place was in darkness. To either side of the house were the outlines of dark evergreen bushes. 'I can't reach the door from here,' I said.

'Course we can't. We go up the drive, stupid.'

'But what if we get caught?'

'We won't get caught. He's about a hundred years old. And he's half-blind.'

'Aye, we know him,' Tim said, 'but old and blind … We can't do that.'

'Yeah, that wouldn't be fair,' I added.

We moved on to the next driveway. Alan shoved me in the back. 'Go on. You first.'

I made my way slowly towards the door. The sound of my feet crunching the gravel seemed to echo up and down the street. I stopped about ten yards short of the target. I was sure I could get it from here. I slid my hand down the front of my sweater and closed my fingers on the first egg. I turned to see where the others were. They were still at the gate, urging me on.

'Hurry up!' Martin whispered. 'We'll keep a look-out.'

I took out the egg, leaned back and took aim.

'Hey! You two!' It was a loud, booming, self-assured voice. I couldn't tell where it came from. It seemed to echo around the darkened end of the street. 'And just what do you think you're doing, eh?'

I turned, clutching the egg in my hand. Alan was out in the road, looking up and down. Tim and Martin were cowering behind the gatepost. I wanted to run, but I didn't know which way. Was this hidden enemy in front of me or behind?

'Stay right where you are. Both of you.'

I still couldn't see anybody. But then there came another sound, a hoarse panting, and scrabbling sound a dog makes when it's tugging at a leash on a gravel drive. A moment later that's precisely what I saw emerging from the shrubbery, a large black dog, teeth bared, front feet off the ground and straining to reach me.

I didn't wait to see who, or what, was on the other end of the lead. I turned and ran, flat out, fully expecting to be leapt on any moment by the monster dog. The others were several paces ahead of me, all of them running like the wind. The question now was, should I turn in at our front gate and let our pursuer know where I lived, or keep running and risk him overtaking us and letting the hound loose?

In the end my mind was made up for me. Right outside the house, as I hesitated, my right foot hit a frozen puddle. Down I went, flat on my front. I lay there for a moment, tensing my body against the expected impact of a dog landing on my back. It never came. The only sounds were the pulsing of my heartbeat in my ears and the fading sound of footsteps as the rest of the gang raced for home. It was only as I eased myself upright that I heard the crackle of crushed shells and felt the cold raw eggs trickling down my stomach and into my underpants.

Back in the house I crept slowly past the living room where the others were clustered round the box watching Mud perform Dynamite. I tiptoed upstairs, my legs bowed outward as the eggs slithered down my thighs. In the privacy of the bedroom I took off my coat, dropped it on the floor and started peeling off the sweater. A mixture of white and yolk plopped onto the floor. More of it clung to my T-shirt. I ripped that off, and my trousers, then gathered up the whole lot and ran to the bathroom, where I hurled them in the wash-basin and turned on the hot tap. Then I grabbed a flannel and started to clean myself.

I came down to the living room for the last few minutes of Top Of The Pops trying to act as if nothing out of the ordinary had happened.

'Why you in your dressing gown already?' Christine asked.

''Cos I felt like it.'

'I thought you were at your friend's house anyway,' she said.

'I was, but I got bored.'

'Oh.' She couldn't have sounded less interested if she'd tried.

It was some time later that Mum went upstairs and discovered my clothes. She shouted from the top of the stairs. 'Just what is the meaning of this, Michael Pannett?'

I went up to face the music. Yes, I'd messed up my clothes but surely she'd be pleased that I'd put them in to soak. I'd seen her do just that a hundred times with Dad's oily overalls. She wasn't pleased. At all. She grabbed my ear and led me to the bathroom.

'Just how do you explain that?' she said.

There in the wash-basin I saw my T-shirt, sweater and trousers sitting in a pool of scalding water and poached eggs, lightly scrambled.

I tried to talk my way out of it. It had worked in the past. I told Mum that Alan had got some hens and they had too many eggs and I'd bought some with my pocket money to help out, since Dad was

always saying how it cost a fortune to feed a family these days and…
My strategy was to keep talking until she couldn't take any more and
begged me to shut up.

I really thought I'd got away with it until next morning when Mum
went to the pantry and counted her eggs. There was no point denying
it. I'd nicked them, and now I was nicked. The challenge was to stop
her banning me from the Guy Fawkes party. As she thought up a suitable punishment I planned a dash to Alan's house to get replacements
from him. Maybe that would settle it. But by some miracle the
thought of a ban never seemed to enter Mum's head. What she wanted was summary justice. And she got it. She took my week's pocket
money from her purse, handed it over and took it straight back. It
was a simple case of, 'You took the eggs, you pay for them.' A week
with no pocket money? It seemed to me I'd got off lightly.

So the Fifth of November dawned under trouble-free skies. There
was only one blot on the landscape.

'How long is it now?' I asked.

Dad was in the garage, sorting out his collection of old tin cans and
filling them with sand. I was loading them onto the wheelbarrow,
ready to be taken down to the bonfire site when it got dark. If it ever
got dark. When it came to health and safety, Dad was well ahead of
the game. He stopped what he was doing and looked at his watch.

'Well,' he said, 'according to my ancient timepiece, I'd say it's four
minutes since you last asked me, making it …' He paused and did
some adding up in his head. 'Let's call it six hours and forty minutes.'

I can't think of another day in the entire calendar that drags like
Guy Fawkes day when you're a child. Waiting for that mound of
wood to be lit and the first of the fireworks to soar into the night sky
was about as bad as waking up in the pitch dark on Christmas morning. Worse, in fact. At least then you could feel the various shapes in
the stocking, listen to the packages rustling and speculate as to what
each might contain. But the Fifth of November? It seemed to go on

and on and on. How grown-ups could say things like, 'Doesn't time fly?' was beyond me.

Somehow we got through the morning. By the time we went for our dinner at one o'clock I was so wound up I'd almost lost my appetite. The afternoon dragged. The clock in the kitchen seemed to go slower and slower. I watched Dad fetch his hammer, some nails, a few lengths of wood and, finally, the big old biscuit tin in which he stored the fireworks. He sent me to fetch Phil and the girls out. Then he opened the lid for us to peek inside, and there they were: bangers, jumping jacks, rockets, Roman candles, some of those special ones with plastic at the end that you were allowed to hold in your hand, a couple of Catherine wheels and of course a packet of sparklers.

I remember standing there, looking at them in silence, almost reverent. I leaned forward and sniffed, long and hard. There's nothing quite like the smell of fireworks – although I knew that tomorrow morning I'd be walking round the field picking up the discarded bangers, sniffing the wonderful smell of spent gunpowder and wondering how I was going to get through another twelve months before I could enjoy once more the greatest day of the year.

By the time we came out of the workshop, Dad holding the biscuit tin, us four all following him, the miracle had happened. It had started getting dark. In the kitchen Mum was setting out the food – not for tea but for the feast that awaited us later on. The Avenue Guy Fawkes party wasn't just about the bonfire and the fireworks; it was about the grub. People brought sausages, pies, potatoes to bake in the embers, all sorts of special grub. Even toffee-apples and flapjacks.

As ever we got a lecture from Dad about safe practice before we left the house. He did it for all the right reasons, but he forgot that we'd had the same lecture at school, several times over. So we listened, and nodded, and agreed that we would not throw fireworks under any circumstances, that we would leave him to set them off, neither would we get too close to him when he was lighting the blue touch-paper, and he made us promise that if a rocket, or any other firework, failed to ignite, we would not approach it.

'There's more children burned on this night than any other day of the year,' he said. 'And we don't want any of your names on the list, do we?'

We agreed that we didn't, and prepared to set off. Between us we had to carry the trays of food, the tins with the sand in, and the bottles of pop – which I pointed out could serve as fire extinguishers in an emergency, especially if you gave them a good shake. The girls had turnip lanterns, and Dad was in charge of the 'ark of the covenant' as Phil called it, the precious biscuit tin. We gave Petra a slap-up meal with extra biscuits in it, shut her in the kitchen with the curtains drawn tight, and set off.

All along the Avenue our neighbours were on their way to the field. We formed a sort of procession, and the kids soon formed up into gangs, comparing notes on the food we'd brought, the firework budgets of our respective families, and our various estimates as to the height of the fire

Each year a different father took a turn at lighting the fire. Whoever it was this year had struck lucky. We'd had a dry autumn, and the weather this night was perfect: still, not too cold, and with a half moon visible behind some thin high clouds. But before the fire could be lit the guy had to be hoisted to the top. That was a job for someone with a ladder. Once he was in position the fun could start. Whoever was in charge had obviously decided to take no chances. You could smell the paraffin from miles away, and as soon as the first match was applied, up it went. After that it was organised chaos, with fireworks going off all over the field, and lots of oohs and aahs as the sky filled with star-bursts, drifts of smoke and an occasional boom.

Fireworks never last long enough. It's a fact of life. No matter how many there are, how expensive they are, how wonderful they are, the show always ends far too soon. But the good part about this was the certainty that, as soon as the show was over and the food had been shared out, the parents would want to get back home to their easy chairs and their tellies. And this night, for the first time in my life, I was allowed to stay behind for an hour or so with Phil and his friends. No sooner had the last adults drifted away than out came Phil's secret supply of fireworks.

'Where'd you get them from?' I asked, as he pulled out a cluster of rockets, a handful of bangers and a tangle of rubber bands.

'Been collecting,' he said. 'For a week or two. Now then, watch this. You're gonna like it.'

With that he used the rubber bands to strap a pair of bangers to a rocket. His mate produced a bottle and a match, and set everything up. We stood back and waited. Whoosh! went the rocket, and just as it disappeared in the sky the bangers started spewing out orange sparks, exploding at the same time as the mother vessel sent out a cluster of silver stars.

'Wow!' I shouted. 'Got any more?'

The lads did indeed, enough for another couple of displays. By now the fire had burned down to a large mound of fierce, red-hot embers, with just the heaviest timbers in the middle still sending out pale orange and blue flames. We popped a couple of foil-wrapped potatoes on the coals. This was living with a capital L. I remembered I still had some sparklers in my pocket, and pulled them out. Phil and his mates called me a big girl, but once I'd lit them at the fire they were happy enough to take one each and draw patterns in the darkness.

Once we'd used them up it was a matter of standing around the fire, waiting for the spuds to cook. Most of the people had gone home, leaving just a few die-hards. Every few minutes we'd reach out with a foot to drag our spuds out of the ashes and see whether they were done. At last it seemed they were, and we rolled them in the grass to cool them off, then blew and blew on them, but we still managed to burn our tongues. Then it was time to make our way home, slowly, reliving the night's best moments and polishing them every time we retold them. By tomorrow, as we revisited the bonfire site and collected up the spent fireworks, we'd be spinning yarns like old men did.

Blood Brothers

Alan held everything steady while I applied the stuff. We had an old paintbrush we'd found in his dad's shed, along with the can of caustic. When I say I applied it, I mean I slapped it on, lathered it. Splish splosh, splish splash. I smothered that pink pony, and rapidly obliterated its curly mane, goofy teeth and daft grin, quite oblivious for the moment to the drops of caustic that were landing on the back of my hand.

'Wow! Look at that!' The ghastly, smirking beast was already melting away, the paint forming little bubbles and ridges and wrinkles. I dipped the brush into the can of Nitromors and slapped some more on.

'Start scraping,' I said. 'Hurry up! I'm burning.'

'Me too.' Alan couldn't wait. A few deft passes with the battered old kitchen knife and the bulk of the offensive image was on the concrete hard standing, a sodden, seething dollop of wrinkled paint and chemicals – on which we promptly knelt as we flicked away the last globules of paint.

'Youch!' We were both on our feet now, hopping about, waving our hands.

'Water!' Alan shouted. 'Quick. It's eating me!'

We hopped across towards the house and turned on the outside tap, holding our hands under it, splashing our knees and filling our shoes with icy cold water. As the pain eased we sat down on the back step and studied the red marks that still stung our hands and knees.

'We could be blood brothers,' I said, inspecting a little spots of clear fluid that had broken out. 'You got any of this?'

'Yeah.' Alan was only half listening. He was crouching low, inspecting the hand-me-down bike that had come from his sister, and before her from their cousin Gavin. It had started out life as a boy's bike, but she'd painted it white and put the pink pony on it. And now it was his. He sat back down beside me and studied his wrist.

'It's like pus,' he said. 'We'll have to be pus brothers Can you have that?'

We hosed the bike down, dowsed our hands once more and studied our handiwork.

'That's better than it was,' I said.

'Still white, though.'

Alan had a point – apart from the patch of bare steel where the late-lamented pony used to be.

'Come on,' I said, 'we'd better put this stuff away before your Dad gets home.'

Once that was done we did the blood brother business, pressing the pockmarked backs of our hands together and sealing our friendship.

I couldn't help feeling sorry for my mate. It was just his misfortune to get the bike the same week that I took delivery of my Raleigh Chopper. I'd got it for my birthday. It was, without question, the biggest and best present I'd ever had in my life up till then, by a mile. Don't get me wrong, we always had good birthdays – and decent presents. One year it was a plastic Six Million Dollar Man; another year it was a six-gun that let off percussion caps. There was a cowboy outfit, an Indian version with fringed trousers and a feathered headdress; there was a space-hopper, and the usual small things like Thunderbirds accessories and, one year, amongst the bigger presents, I remember a set of Klackers that drove everybody nuts.

Looking back, I can see how clever Mum and Dad were. Your present would almost always be something you wanted. But you had to be careful in the way you went about making it known that you wanted it. Subtle, you might say. You were absolutely not allowed to ask for something directly. That was fatal. As we were once told in Sunday school, 'Those who ask don't get, and those who don't ask don't want.' No, if you'd set your heart on some new toy you had to talk about it, casually, over the tea-table, and maybe mention in passing that one of your friends had one – or was getting one for his birthday. However, that particular year all the rules went out of the window. Dad had got a promotion at work, so we were all treated to a special present. And this time we were allowed to 'make suggestions'. I only had one, and that was the Chopper.

Of course, when I first wheeled it out onto Park Avenue and rode it up and down, practising wheelies, all the lads came out to admire it. It truly was a thing of beauty. Not that Petra noticed that. Used as she was to chasing any cyclist who happened to pass the house, she automatically started snapping at my ankles until it dawned on her who it was. The bike was orange, with lots of gleaming chrome. It had extended handlebars, a fake leather high-backed seat and a fancy five-speed gear-shift. The front wheel was smaller than the rear one. Cool? You bet it was. All it needed was an engine and it could've been a motorbike – and didn't I know it. It didn't take long for the other kids to become envious. I suppose they became ashamed of their own bikes, which looked so hopelessly antiquated in comparison. Before long complaints reached our ears that Dad had put all the local parents under pressure. It was true. He had. While I badgered all my friends to go out on rides with me, none of them had anything that could hold a candle to my machine. Suddenly, everybody else's bike looked shabby, clunky and hopelessly out of date. I had set a trend. Who would follow? Alan did his best, bombarding his parents with requests. But they drove a hard bargain. What was wrong with a proper sturdy bike with good old-fashioned Sturmey-Archer three-speed gearing, they asked him? Like the one his sister had handed on to him. If he really wanted one of these daft new things, well, maybe they'd think about it. But only if he stumped up half the cost.

'But they're about thirty pounds!' he complained. 'That means I've got to find... loads of money.'

'Fifteen quid,' I told him. Arithmetic was never Alan's best subject.

'That's a fortune,' he said, but when he said as much to his parents they simply replied, 'All the more reason why you have to show willing.'

While the other kids steered clear of me – or rather of my bike – Alan stood by me. As the summer holidays kicked off, and with his birthday but two weeks away, he agreed to take up my challenge and see how far we could cycle, across the fields and out into the countryside.

We were hot, and we were miles from home. Not so many miles, I suppose, when I look at the map now, but for a couple of eight-year-olds forty years ago it seemed as though we'd already made an epic journey. We'd taken our bikes all the way through the village of Huntington and out to Strensall, entering what was to us another world altogether. We cycled slowly past the army barracks, stopping to gaze at the dark green trucks and half-tracks through a mesh fence topped with barbed wire. We watched as detachments of men in camouflage outfits marched to and fro across the hot tarmac, their drill-sergeant's orders echoing off the walls of the residential blocks. Not for the first time we decided we would have careers as soldiers, with uniforms and guns, and artillery practice with real live ammunition out on Strensall common. We'd blow things up and get paid for it. Heaven.

After standing with our faces pressed to the fence for some time, we remembered how thirsty we were. We made our way to the little shop in the village, pooled what was left of our pocket money and bought a big bottle of dandelion and burdock. That left us with a solitary two-pence piece between us. We shared the drink, taking one glug at a time, then tossed the coin to see who got to drain the last few drops. Then we pedalled on through the woods to the point where the railway line approaches the road. Beyond us lay the common, and the artillery ranges, all covered in heather and dotted with birch trees, between which, we knew, were boggy holes full of moss, frogs and cold water.

Me, aged nine years four months, taken at New Earswick Primary School. Just look at that haircut!

Me, aged twelve.

Me and my siblings in the late 1960s, sporting the new coats that Grandpa had bought us: Phil at the back, me at the front, Auntie Hilda with Gillian on her knee, and Christine on the right.

Dad

Mum

Honk, my pet pig.

Just some of the family menagerie.

My first taste of stardom –
appearing on the children's
TV series *Why Don't You?*.

Petra, our beloved family pet.

'Come on,' I said, straddling my Chopper and turning it towards the gravelled road that led on to undiscovered places, let's see how far we can go.' It was still only mid-afternoon and the sun was high, just a few puffy white clouds blown across an otherwise blue sky by a cooling breeze.

Alan wasn't so sure. He was getting saddle-sore already, or so he said. The real problem, of course, was his bike.

The Scarborough train rattled past, but we hardly even noticed it. If we'd had a few coins left we would've put a couple on the line, but all we had was the two pence piece, and for some reason it seemed important to hang onto that.

Alan was right down in the dumps. 'Where am I gonna find fifteen quid?'

For the first time since my birthday I felt guilty about my good fortune. And I felt sorry for my mate. I looked at the road, winding across the common, and thought of the adventures we might have if we got to the other side. Then I looked at Alan, hands in his pockets, kicking stones at the despised hand-me-down bike.

'Come on,' I said, 'let's head for home.'

We were now pedalling into the breeze, and even for me it was hard work. The truth about the Chopper was, it wasn't a touring bike. At all. If Alan had stopped to think about it, he would've realised he was better off right now. We stopped by the side of the golf course, under a tree, and took a breather. About fifty yards away, on the other side of a fence, three old fellows in brightly coloured sweaters were waiting their turn to tee off. They were all smoking We watched as the first one bent down to place his ball on a tee. He threw away his cigarette, took a couple of practice swings, said something to his friends, then composed himself.

'How far d'you reckon they can they hit a golf ball?' Alan asked.

'Oh, miles,' I said. 'Sometimes they get a hole in one. Or hit a pigeon. They call that a birdie.'

The fellow raised his club, gave an almighty swing. He missed the ball completely and swore. Alan sniggered. 'D'you hear that?' he said. The guy took another swing, and this time he connected. We heard it, loud and clear. All three of them turned and looked in our direction. At first we didn't understand. Then there was a loud 'clunk' just above us as the ball hit the tree and bounced onto the grass where it came to rest, like an egg on a clean bed of straw.

'Blimey!' Alan said. 'That could've hit us.'

He was about to go and pick it up when I grabbed his arm.

'Hang about,' I said.

'What's up?'

'Just hang about, that's all.'

The old gent who'd sliced his shot had his hand to his forehead. He and his mates were all looking our way.

'People pay for golf balls,' I said. 'Secondhand ones, I mean. They're dead valuable. Cost a bomb when they're new.'

The golfers were waving at us and shouting.

'What they saying?' Geoff asked.

'Dunno,' I said, and waved back.

'Well, why don't we give him his ball back?'

''Cos there's a fence. We aren't allowed over it. And like I said … you know, finders keepers. This is public property.'

'Yeah, but we could throw it.'

I didn't answer. I was watching the golfers. The guy who'd sliced his shot reached into his pocket, placed a new ball on the tee and started again. After they'd all teed off, as they were all walking down the fairway towards the next green, I picked the ball up. 'Must be worth five pence, I said. Maybe ten.'

'Two bob?' Alan's eyes widened as he spoke. We were still getting used to decimal currency that year, trying to work out which sounded more impressive, two shillings or ten pence.

'Tell you what,' I said, 'let's have a look around. I bet loads of balls get hit over the fence.'

We must have spent the next hour or so combing the grass between the roadside and the fence. Between us we found a dozen.

'What we gonna do with them?'

'Flog 'em, of course.'

'Who to? It's got to be grown-ups, hasn't it?'

'Good point,' I said. I had a think. 'Does your Dad play?'

Alan shook his head. 'But me uncle does. Maybe we could try him.'

'Yeah, we'll try your uncle.'

I looked out over the course. The three old golfers had long since disappeared and the place seemed deserted. I walked over to the fence, ducked down and slid underneath the wire.

'Come on,' I said, beckoning Alan to follow me. 'There'll be loads more in here, in all this long grass. I bet people lose balls all the time.'

I was right. There were loads. And more loads. By the time we cycled home we each had our pockets filled and the rest of our collection stuffed down our T-shirts, which were firmly tucked inside our trousers.

Next day we were back, scouring the perimeter of the course, ducking under the fence once more when nobody was looking. We kept it up for a week, by which time there couldn't have been a lost ball unaccounted for in the entire parish of Strensall – and to tell the truth, if there had been we couldn't have been bothered. We were confident we had enough. And so, on a Saturday morning we trudged around to Alan's uncle's place, each of us lugging a plastic carrier-bag full of balls. His uncle weeded out a few misshapen ones, a couple of cut and dented ones, and took a dozen or so at fifteen pence apiece. From there, flushed with the thrill of making a sale, we cycled over to the golf course and set up shop outside the clubhouse. By the end of the day we'd got a small mountain of loose change and couple of pound notes, giving us a grand total of twenty-eight pounds.

'Wow, that's fourteen quid each.' I nudged Alan in the ribs. 'Fourteen quid!'

We stood there a few moments, stunned. Neither of us had ever had anything like that much money. We'd never possessed a pound note either, and now we had one each. We felt them, turned them over, examined the pattern, the portrait of the Queen, the signature of the Governor of the Bank of England. Another job I wouldn't mind – although I soon changed my mind on that. As Alan pointed out, signing pound notes day after day couldn't be much fun. He shovelled his coins into his trouser pocket, thought for a moment, then started doing some adding up. 'So this means …' he began.

'Yeah, fantastic. You only need another pound now and you can get your Chopper.' He looked at me, and I looked at him. 'Tell you what,' I said, 'You take fifteen and I'll have the rest.'

'Really?'

'Yeah, really. We're blood brothers, aren't we?'

Just Hanging About

'You know what they come here for, don't you?'

We were sheltering under the lych-gate. Me and Kev, just the two of us. He was carrying a bamboo cane he'd picked up in the churchyard. After a hot afternoon the thunder-clouds had gathered and a few large drops of rain had started to lay the dust. We'd been to the chippy after choir practice, but although we'd eaten our chips and drunk a can of pop we were in no hurry to get home. By this time Mum and Dad had relaxed their rules. I could stay out after tea so long as I got back before dark. We had another half an hour, at least. And if it rained properly, well so what, we'd just get wet.

'Well, do you? Do you know?'

I pondered Kev's question. I wanted to tell him I knew the answer, but the fact was I hadn't a clue what he was getting at. He was a year ahead of me in school – and, if I was to believe all his boasts, about three years ahead in life experience. It was all thanks to that brother of his. Several years older than us and, as Mum once remarked, 'altogether too forward'.

'Necking. They come here for necking and that,' Kev said. 'You know, lads with their girlfriends. Having a snog. Kissy-kissy.'

'Yeah, I know.' Sometimes I found Kev's superior attitude a bit insulting. As if I didn't know what necking was.

'Yeah,' he said, 'you bring a girl here she has to kiss you. It's a tradition.'

When Kev made a statement of fact, you were expected to take it as the Gospel truth – whether you believed it or not.

'But why?' I said. The place seemed a bit dingy to me, not at all romantic. 'Why here?'

He looked up at the timbers, heavy with dust and cobwebs. Reaching up he poked at the remains of a swallow's nest with the cane and brought down a light shower of pale dry mud.

'It's traditional, like I said. In the old days, see, girls weren't allowed to kiss fellows – not till they got married. They never had the back row of the flicks like we do. Or youth clubs, or owt like that. So they came here. To the kissing-gate. Still do, as a matter of fact. Me brother brings all his girlfriends here.'

He pulled out two more cans of pop and handed me one.

'Cheers,' I said, then asked, 'You seen them?'

'Sure I have. You can get a ringside seat. Look.'

He clambered onto the top of the gate, swung his legs up and there he was, perched in the timbers that supported the pitched roof, his feet dangling.

'Come on up,' he said. 'You sit here you can spy on people. I do it all the time. Seen all sorts, me. Grab a few stones and get yourself up here.'

'Stones? What do I want them for?'

'You'll see. I got some in my pocket. You need some of your own.'

I did as he said – you always did what Kev said – and then tried to climb up to where he was. It was harder work than it looked, but I made it – and just in time. As I squirmed my way into position, hunched down with my head touching the rough timbers of the roof, Kev nudged me and pressed a finger to his lips. Footsteps were approaching. We caught sight of an elderly couple, walking arm in arm. The old man was unfurling an umbrella, not that it was raining properly yet. Kev winked at me, took out a stone and held it between his thumb and forefinger. I wondered if they were going to start kissing. It seemed to me they were a bit old for it. Then, as they walked beneath us, Kev dropped his first stone. It didn't hit them, just pinged off the ground. They half-stopped, looked at it and walked on. He threw another after them, and they stopped again, looked around, and carried on, muttering to each other.

We waited a few minutes and supped at our cans. Thunder rumbled in the background. We couldn't tell whether it was coming nearer or not.

'Count to five,' Kev said.

'Why?'

'Oh no, that's after the lightning and before the thunder. Tells you how many miles away it is.'

'I haven't seen any lightning, have you?'

'Nah.' There was a pause. I drained my can and crushed it the way I'd seen Phil do it.

'Sh! Here comes someone.' Kev was suddenly alert, listening.

A woman was walking her dog, on a lead. As she passed underneath us, we both dropped a stone. One landed on the ground, the other hit the dog. It barked. The woman told it to shush, and tugged on its lead. As she tried to walk on Kev lobbed another stone. The dog turned and looked right at us, and snarled.

'Oh, don't be silly George!' The woman tugged on the leash and dragged the dog away.

'George!' I couldn't help laughing. 'What kind of name's that?'

But Kev wasn't listening. He had his finger over his mouth again, his head cocked to one side. I heard the slow heavy tread of a youth and the click-clack click-clack of someone with a shorter, faster stride. There was a bit of whispering too, and a giggle.

I held my breath and waited. The footsteps came closer, then slowed down. Kev tapped me on the knee and winked.

It was Steve, his big brother. He was fifteen, a tall lad with lots of wavy hair, flared jeans and a multi-coloured tank top. His girlfriend was shorter. She too had flares on, and high-heeled shoes.

I looked at Kev and he looked at me, raising his eyebrows. We both looked down at the newly arrived couple. They weren't hanging about. They were in a clinch, arms around each other in a passionate embrace. Kev was trying not to laugh – and barely succeeding. His whole body was shaking. I could feel it through the timbers, and was sure that they were going to start rattling. But if they did, Steve and his girlfriend were oblivious. They got on with the business in hand while we tightened our grip on the beams.

I gesticulated to Kev. His frown framed the question, 'What?'

The fact was, after all that pop I needed the toilet, and his brother showed no signs of going home any time soon. In fact, he and his girl had now sat down, and he'd taken out his cigarettes. How long was this going to take? My legs were starting to go numb, and my bladder was aching. And what if they saw us? All they had to do was glance upwards. For the moment, mercifully, they only seemed to have eyes for each other.

I squeezed my legs together and pulled a face. Steve stood up. Surely this was the moment. We were going to be discovered and he'd haul us down and beat us to a pulp. I'd heard all kinds of stories about Steve – mostly from Kev, of course. But who cared if he'd exaggerated? The guy was huge. I watched through half-closed eyes as he stretched his arms, outwards and upwards. I could easily have reached down and plucked the cigarette from his hand. The smoke was tickling my nose, making me want to sneeze.

And then, just when I thought there was no hope, came the miracle. From far away we heard a police siren, approaching rapidly. Next thing we could see blue flashes lighting up the sky.

'What's going on?'

It was the girl who spoke. She was on her feet and out from under us. Steve got up and followed her onto the path. All I could see now were their legs, a few yards away. Why don't they go and look, I thought. Go on. See what's happening, before I burst. Wherever the police car was, it seemed to have come to a standstill. The siren had stopped but lazy blue flashes were still flickering across the dusty timbers around us.

'Come on, let's have a look. Might be an accident.' As the girl spoke I saw her feet disappear and then, the miracle I'd been praying for: Steve followed her down the path.

Kev and I didn't need to say a word. We dropped, turned and ran the other way, past the gravestones and around the back of the church, where he headed for home and I propped myself against the wall beside Charlotte Elizabeth Richardson and did what I had to do.

We didn't try spying on people again after that. Kev told me that he and his girlfriend had started hanging out there, and if he ever caught me watching him he'd have me. Did I understand? Yes, Kev. What else could I say?

A Moving Experience

Dad was in a good mood. Not that he was ever very grumpy – just quiet, and not a man to show his feelings; but on this day he seemed to be especially cheerful, almost playful. He folded up his newspaper, got up from the breakfast table and winked at Mum, then said, 'Come on, you lot. Let's get this cleared away. We're going for a drive. It's a magical mystery tour.'

He had an odd sort of look on his face, as if he was trying not to grin.

It was a sunny April morning, and as I took a pile of dirty dishes to the sink I wondered whether he was planning a trip over to Staintondale, to the farm. Once the Easter holidays came that was always on the agenda.

'Come on, where we going?' Christine asked.

'Aha. That's for us to know and you to find out,' Mum said. I could tell from the way she spoke that this was a special treat of some sort. Like Dad, she had a sort of half smile on her face. 'Come along. Don't just stand there trying to guess,' she said. 'Best way to find out is to get this kitchen tidied up and get in that car.'

When the parents were in this kind of mood there was no problem at all in getting us to do as they said. Something good was in the air, and we couldn't wait to find out what it was. We hurried through our chores, but made sure we did them properly. No skiving, no cutting corners. Everything done as it should be.

'Right,' Dad said. We were all in our places in the back of the Traveller. Everybody was watching Dad. Nobody was arguing. Not even me –

despite the fact that Gillian had spread her doll's clothes all over my seat yet again. 'Everybody ready?'

'Yes.'

'Everybody sitting comfortably?'

'Yes.' The tension was unbearable. When would he tell us what was going on? 'Right then, let this journey into the unknown begin.'

We knew that Dad could keep this up all day if he wanted to. With Mum, if you wheedled and pestered her long enough she'd usually crack, out of sheer exasperation. Anything for a bit of peace and quiet. But not Dad. He would set his face in that half smile and blandly ignore you. You'd find out what was going on when he thought it was time for you to find out. There was absolutely no point trying to winkle it out of him.

We drove on in silence. We were heading away from York and out into the country. Christine nudged me and whispered, 'Helmsley. I think we're heading to Helmsley.'

'What's there?'

She shrugged. 'Shops. A lot of old buildings.' That didn't sound too exciting to me. 'And a ruined castle,' she added. That was more like it.

'Are we going to see the White Horse again?' Gillian asked.

We'd been for an outing there the previous summer, picking wild bilberries on the top of the hill, with the gliders taking off over our heads. I watched Mum and Dad to see whether they were going to respond. I might as well have been watching a couple of statues.

Pretty soon we came to Easingwold. Was this our destination? It didn't look very enticing – apart from a fish and chip shop in the market-place.

'Nearly there,' Dad said.

We were through the market place already and heading out into the country once more. We passed fields where lambs were jumping around in the grass, hedgerows splashed with patches of vivid white blossom. There were one or two fields of something bright yellow, vivid in the sunlight. Dad told us it was a new crop called oil-seed rape.

'They make oil out of it,' he said, 'for cooking. Better for you than lard,' he added.

I tried to imagine how they could turn a plant into oil, but gave up. Looking out of the window I saw that we were starting to climb. We passed a cricket pitch to one side, then we entered a village.

Phil read the sign on the side of the road. 'Crayke,' he said. 'What kind of name's that?'

I looked around. At the centre of the village there was a corner shop on one side of the road, a pub on the other – the Durham Ox.

'It's one of the oldest villages in England,' Mum said.

'It is indeed,' Dad said. 'Crayke. It's a venerable name. It comes from an ancient Celtic word meaning crag or outcrop.'

None of us spoke. What was there to say? Dad seemed to have an answer for everything. I was always amazed at how much knowledge he had. But whenever I asked him where he got it all from he said that it was a simple matter of taking the trouble to find things out. If ever a question came up to which he didn't know the answer, he said, he'd look it up in one of his many books. And if it wasn't there he'd go to the library and find a book that would supply the answer. He spent a lot of his spare time with his head in a book. He'd studied long and hard, right up until he was thirty, to become a chartered mechanical engineer – and he continued to study in his own time for years and years. He said it was the best way to get ahead in life.

'All right, children – here we are.'

Dad had stopped the car on the main street and switched off the engine. I looked out. What kind of outing was this? I was hoping to see a shop selling sticky rock, or beach-balls, or maybe a café, a play-ground, perhaps a view of the sea. But no, we were on an ordinary village road and we were parked outside a large brick house. Paint was peeling from the front door. The windows looked grimy. One was cracked. There were no curtains.

Dad opened the driver's door and got out.

Mum unbuckled her safety belt. 'Come on,' she said, 'come and have a look at your new home.'

That got us out of our seats. 'New home?' we chorused. 'What new home?'

'Ah well,' Dad said as we all emerged from the car, our eyes darting from the house to him and back again. 'We thought we'd surprise you.'

Mum laughed. 'Looks as though you've managed that pretty well, Jeff. Look at them. Stunned.'

Dad took a bunch of keys from his pocket and unlocked the front door. That's when I saw the sign, the name of the place: Beech House.

'You mean we're going to come and live here?' Phil said.

'Yes.'

'Wow. When?'

'Not for a while yet. There are a few repairs to do first. You'll see,' he added. 'But it won't be long.'

Dad explained that after gaining the last of the qualifications he'd studied for, he'd got a promotion at work and been given a pay-rise. And that meant that we could afford a bigger house. 'And a chance to live in the countryside,' Mum added. Then she nudged Christine and said, 'There's a couple of fields out the back. Paddocks.'

'Oh wow! You mean me and Gillian can have a pony? That'd be fantastic.'

Mum smiled and stepped into the house. 'I don't see why not,' she said.

We followed her through the doorway. The place was gloomy and cold. It couldn't have been decorated in years, and it smelt damp and musty. But it seemed huge, and full of possibilities. It could almost have been a castle.

'Of course,' Dad said, 'it wants a few improvements. A heating system for a start.'

'And a proper bathroom,' Mum said. 'And a kitchen, rather than that old scullery.'

Dad said that until he got the heating sorted out we'd be burning wood, as it was cheap. It meant that Phil and I would have to learn to swing an axe to split logs. It all sounded very exciting. We walked along the hallway, the bare floorboards creaking.

'Not haunted is it?' Phil asked.

Behind me I heard Gillian give a little squeak of fear, and Phil stifled a laugh.

'Now, don't go upsetting your sister,' Mum said. She turned to Gillian. 'Of course it's not haunted. You brother's just being silly. There's no such thing as – ' She stopped short of saying the actual word. Everybody was excited enough as it was.

As we went round the house it seemed more and more likely to me that it could be home to all manner of other-worldly beings. As well as the general gloominess there were damp patches on the walls, rotten bits on the skirting boards, and cobwebs everywhere. In the scullery was an old iron range, some bare wooden cupboards, and one of those things you hang your washing on to dry and pull up to the ceiling. In the corners were old mousetraps. In the pantry there were vicious-looking metal hooks in the ceiling – for hanging up hams, according to Mum.

We looked around, then climbed the stairs, gripping a wooden handrail that wobbled and shook. There was a tiny, ancient bathroom with an enamelled tub and yellow tiles on the wall. There were four bedrooms. We walked into one at the front of the house that faced the road.

'We thought this would do for you boys,' Mum said.

There were a couple of old bedsteads. One had a pile of broken plaster and what looked like an old bird's nest on it. Above it was a hole in the ceiling. The walls seemed to have several layers of wallpaper, some of it peeling off.

'Don't worry,' Dad said. 'We'll soon get rid of all the rubbish and fix the place up. By the time we're done you won't recognise it.'

I think Mum and Dad could see that we found the house a little spooky. They took us outside, and that lifted our mood immediately. Outside consisted of a long garden, a collection of outbuildings and a field. The field was divided into two halves by a thorn hedge. Partway down was a pond.

'Look at it,' Dad said. 'There's seven acres there. That's a lot of land. Picture York City's pitch. It'd fit in here ... ooh, three or four times. There's enough garden for us to grow all our fruit and vegetables, and of course I'll put up a greenhouse.'

'Can we have chickens?' I said.

'Chickens, geese, goats, cats, ducks. You can have what you like so long as you're prepared to look after them.'

Just to show us what seven acres meant, Dad walked us down to the end of the field and back. Gillian and Christine spent the whole time planning for the ponies they were going to have, what colour they would be and what they'd be called and which outbuilding they'd live in and what they'd eat . . . and in the end Mum had to tell them to calm down. Needless to say, her words had no effect.

By the time moving day came, several weeks later, Mum and Dad had tidied the place up and made it habitable. By the time we'd moved our furniture in and I'd put my Thunderbirds poster up on the bedroom wall it started to feel a bit like home.

It's Dark in Here

If moving-in day seemed chaotic, it also seemed like fun. With all the furniture piled up in corners of the various rooms while Mum and Dad made up their minds where it would go, every room was an adventure playground. There were stacks of boxes all over the place. We'd been collecting them for weeks from the shops, and Dad had been bringing them home from work. He'd also got a number of tea-chests with exotic writing stamped on the side – Chinese in some cases. Mum had put a label on each one, but there were so many of them piled up that it was impossible to find everything without pulling half the pile down – which led to further confusion. Mercifully, Mum had got the food organised – so we at least didn't go hungry.

Bedtime seemed fun at first, with me and Phil arranging our things in the room we were to share, having a wrestling match over who got the bed by the window – the elder of us, naturally – then turning our attention to the girls in the room next door. We started by bombarding them with scrunched-up clothes from the cardboard boxes we'd brought upstairs, and of course it soon turned into a massive pillow-fight.

Mum and Dad were unusually calm about all the running up and down the landing, the shrieking and thumping. I think they were too tired to get angry, just relieved to be inside their dream home at last. Instead of shouting at us they called us all down to the kitchen for a hot drink and a biscuit, and there we sat, gasping from the battle, surrounded by boxes of china, pots and pans, a basket full of laundry, the table all piled high with bread, vegetables and other foodstuffs.

By the time we'd downed a mug of cocoa each, sitting on the wooden chairs, tucking our feet under the rails to avoid contact with the bare stone floor, we were all starting to feel the effects of the day. We trudged up the stairs, picking the bits of fluff and feathers out of our T-shirts, changed into our pyjamas and climbed into our beds. Mum and Dad came up to wish us a good first night in our new home. Before she put the light out, Mum reminded us that our first job next day would be to sweep up all the feathers we'd scattered across the landing. Then she put out the light, and swung the door to. It closed with a resounding clunk. That's when an awful realisation hit me.

Back in Park Avenue, the bedroom was pretty dark, but never exactly pitch-black. There were one or two street lights along the Avenue, and once your eyes had got accustomed to the night you could always make out the shape of the chest-of-drawers, the tall wardrobe, the outline of the window, even on the blackest night with the curtains drawn tight. And every so often a car would go by the school at the top of the road, its headlights piercing the gap by the curtain rail and sweeping across the ceiling to illuminate the room for a few moments and cast weird shadows. Out here in Crayke there was nothing – just a tiny chink of light at the bottom of the door. But a few minutes later, as Mum and Dad tiptoed up to bed I heard the creak of their bedroom door opening, then the click as they flipped the brass switch and extinguished the landing light. Suddenly it was like being in a coal cellar at midnight.

'Phil!' I whispered.

No answer.

'Phil!'

'Yeah, what is it?' he mumbled from deep under his blankets.

'It's dark.'

'Course it's dark, you prat. It's night-time.'

'No,' I said, 'really, really dark. I can't see anything at all.'

'Well, what do you want to see?'

'I don't know. Something. I don't like this.'

I could hear Phil throw back his blankets and sigh. 'You'll get used to it,' he said. 'It takes twenty minutes for your night vision to come through.'

'How do you know?'

'How do I know what?'

'About night vision.'

''Cos I read things. In books. Now shut up, will you?'

I lay there, sweating with fear, alive to every creak and murmur in the old house, straining to hear any sounds other than Phil's gentle snoring. What if Mum and Dad had moved us into a house that was haunted? Old houses could be haunted, couldn't they? So should I stay awake and risk seeing a ghost, or go to sleep and run the even greater danger of being taken off into the spirit world, a place of demons and monsters?

A brief rattling noise from outside was followed by the hoot of an owl, sending me deep down the bed, clutching my pillow. It sounded as though it was in the room with us. I stayed down there as long as I could, every little creak now sounding like the footsteps of an imagined giant who only had one thing on his mind – to find me.

It was hot down there, stifling, but I didn't dare come out in case ... After a few minutes my need for air became desperate. I popped my head out. Maybe my night vision would have kicked in. But after three or four attempts I still couldn't see a thing. Maybe I should've eaten my carrots, I thought, like Mum told me. Or was it the greens? One of them made you see in the dark. And one made your hair curl – but which one was it? Maybe I'd have to eat both, to be sure. Even though I hated them.

I must have got to sleep in the end, because I remember waking up, twice, and on each occasion I heard the floorboards creak, right outside the door. Once I was certain I heard a door opening. I lay there rigid, trying to still the thumping of my heart, sure that it would alert the ghostly intruder to my presence. I called for Phil, but he was miles away, deep in slumber.

And then, as the cocoa worked its way through my system and got to work with the anxiety and fear, I realised I wanted the toilet. But that was all the way downstairs, and nothing would induce me to venture on that journey. I lay there for what seemed like hours. I heard a cockerel crow somewhere in the village. I heard a vehicle making its way up the main street, stopping and starting. Then the clinking of milk bottles. Surely it would be light soon, and it would be safe to go down to the toilet? Just as I thought I would burst, just as the faintest light started to show around the edge of the curtains, I heard Mum and Dad's door open, and the pad-pad-pad of footsteps as one of them went down to put a kettle on.

I got out of bed and hurried out onto the landing, then down the stairs.

'What's up? Couldn't you sleep?'

It was Dad, putting a lighted match to the camping stove. As he'd explained to us before the move, the house had old-fashioned wiring that required round-pin plugs. He'd been collecting them in the months leading up to the move, but he still had to change them all over. Until then, the electric kettle was out of action.

I scuttled out to the privy – and immediately wished I'd stopped to put my slippers on. It was icy cold out there, and the floor was bare concrete.

'Yes,' Dad said when I returned, 'there's a lot needs doing.'

I was making my way to the door, my teeth chattering. I wanted to hurry back to bed where it was warm.

'Always the same with an old house. Full of cobwebs.' He sighed as he dipped his finger in the pan of water he'd set on the Primus. 'Cobwebs,' he repeated. 'And the ghosts of previous occupants.'

I stopped in my tracks. 'Ghosts?' I said. 'You mean this place is haunted?'

Dad laughed. 'No,' he said. 'I just mean that the people who lived here in the past – well, they all leave their mark. And now it's our turn to leave ours. New wiring, a heating system, new plumbing.' Then he added, 'But if this place is peopled by ghosts – well, I'm afraid they're not going to be happy when they see what I've got in store.'

With that he went outside himself, leaving me to dash upstairs and dive under the covers.

Some time later, after we'd got properly settled in, somebody told us the story that everybody in the village knew. It seemed that our new home was built on the site of an older house that had burned down, killing the two occupants. When Gillian heard this she surprised us all by telling all her friends that her room was haunted, that she could hear it breathing at night. Her new friends were soon queuing up to stay overnight with her. As for me, I tried hard to forget what I'd heard. It made me very nervous at night.

I'm Freezing

Midwinter, that first year, conjures up memories of the weekly wash hanging over a clothes-horse in front of an open fire; of a white frost painting pictures all over the bedroom windows; of a queue of children waiting for the kettle to boil so that they could fill their nightly hot-water bottles; of coming downstairs in the morning to find the dishcloth frozen fast to the draining board. It makes me shiver just to think of it, and of course it's more or less unimaginable today.

But when we moved into Beech House Farm the very idea of having a radiator in your bedroom or a heated towel-rail in the bathroom – well, it was a fantasy. You might have seen something like it on the telly – along with glamorous housewives traipsing across a bathroom carpeted with what looked like a polar bear's coat – but you dismissed it out of hand. It was what posh people had, or Americans.

We never imagined that we might live in such luxury. Flying cars, time machines, inter-stellar travel: we could envisage all that, no problem. It was there in our weekly comics. But a North Yorkshire winter without chilblains and frozen milk? Don't be daft.

Dad, however, was different. As ever.

Dad, you see, was a brain-box. No two ways about that. He used long words, he read books, and he studied all kinds of technology. He carried out strange experiments in his workshop and did calculations on the back of his newspaper at the breakfast table while tut-tutting at us lot for arguing over the last piece of toast.

His forehead was broad and high. He was nicknamed Christopher Lee, because he really did look ever so slightly like that master of the macabre. I suppose a later generation would've called him Max Headroom. He was a thinker. And, like most thinkers, he demanded peace and quiet. Fat chance of finding any of that in our house, with four children, various pets, and half the kids in the neighbourhood swarming around the place. No wonder he spent so much time in the workshops and outbuildings.

We'd moved up to Crayke in the springtime. Life was easy. When summer came we ate picnic lunches outside, played cricket in the fields until it got dark, then slumped into our beds, hot and exhausted, threw the blankets off and flung the windows wide open. Winter was the last thing on our minds.

But all through those carefree weeks before we went back to school, Dad was plotting. He knew that winter would come, and he knew very well what might be in store. And so he devised a plan – a plan which, just like the rest of his projects, would take months to evolve, many more months to become a reality.

His grand plan to install a central heating system of his own design and built by his own endeavours would come to pass – but not before we'd suffered a long, snowy winter in a huge, draughty house – made all the more draughty by the holes he started knocking in the walls, floors and ceilings.

After the initial excitement, we kids didn't pay a lot of attention to what was going on. We got used to seeing him tap at the old lead pipes that ran up through the kitchen, or crouch down under the sink to examine the rising main, or stand like a statue, staring up at the outside brickwork, jotting occasionally in a little black notebook. We became accustomed to looking up from the kitchen and seeing the underside of Christine's bed. We thought nothing of Dad suddenly leaving the tea-table and prising up a floorboard to probe the dark space beneath with an old screwdriver in one hand and a flickering torch in the other. We accepted his frequent disappearances, up the rickety ladder and through the little hatch that led to the attic.

At first I was curious. Despite being told not to, I followed him up one time and stuck my head into the dark, dusty, cobwebby roof-space to see what was up there. I was hoping for long-lost cabin-trunks full of treasure. There was little to see but darkness, dust and cobwebs, as well as a few sagging rafters.

But the sight that sticks in my kind is of Dad's rear end as he went from beam to beam on his hands and knees, coughing through the handkerchief he wore around his nose and mouth, his torch illuminating the underside of the slates and, on one occasion, a huge old wasps' nest.

Yes, we were roused to interest the time his foot came through the ceiling and into our bedroom on an August night, but by and large we ignored him. We let him get on with it. He was just being Dad, and we were used to that.

The much-discussed heating project seemed about as realistic as his plans for growing tomatoes by hydroponics in the greenhouse he had yet to build, as remote to us as the work he did at Vickers, developing a new laser sighting system for the next generation of tanks for the British Army. Once or twice he brought home a laser device from work and showed us how powerful it was. He'd hand me his binoculars so that I could focus on some far-distant tree and watch the little red light dart about as he tried to hold the torch steady in his hand.

When winter came it came with a bang. The north wind blew, the top of the chimney collapsed, knocking a couple of slates off the roof, and – to our delight and amazement – allowing snow to cascade into the corner of our bedroom through the hole Dad had cut there in order to accommodate the flue for the boiler he would install 'when time and money permitted'. The fact that the snow didn't melt, that Phil and I shaped it into a miniature snowman that lasted three full days, tells you all you need to know about the temperature inside our room. It was f-f-freezing.

Mum, bless her, did her best to see that we kept dry and warm. She piled extra blankets on the beds and even loaned us an ancient fur coat which she'd dragged out of a trunk. It had belonged to her own grandmother and would one day, she assured us, come back into fashion. Trying to get to sleep under the unblinking gaze of the dead fox that formed the coat's collar, I asked myself why anyone would want such a thing. But we didn't complain. In that bitter winter every little helped.

Of course we had hot-water-bottles too, and that was where the trouble started. Every night we took it in turns to fill the kettle, heat it up on the old gas stove and pour the contents carefully into our rubber bottles. Every night Mum would remind us not to boil the water. 'It'll perish the rubber,' she said. I'm sure she was also worried about our own safety, but she never mentioned that. Just the rubber. Of course, being about nine or ten by this the time I didn't need telling. I knew better. My feet had been so cold in bed during the freeze-up that night after night I'd raised the temperature. Sure, it made the bottle too hot to handle, but this is where I'd been clever. Far too clever for my own good, in the end. Every night when I brought it down and emptied out the previous night's water, I also brought down an old blanket that I'd found in a drawer in the landing. Wrapping the hottie in that, I could fill it with water hot enough to brew tea, and it kept my feet cosy right through the night.

Then came the evening when Phil was away, sleeping over at his mate's house. The weather still had an icy grip on North Yorkshire, and the bedroom was as cold as ever. I know, I thought, I'll use Phil's bottle too. Phil's was different from mine. It had a different type of stopper. But I didn't know that. Why would I? And how would I know that I'd not got it in place securely? When I got into bed and kicked it to one side is the answer.

The yelp I let out as the scalding water hit my foot brought everybody – Mum, Dad, the girls and Petra – to my door. They found me hopping about on one leg, tears streaming down my cheeks, and my foot a livid red.

'What on earth have you done?' Mum's face was contorted with worry and perplexity.

Dad had pulled the blankets back to reveal the now empty hottie. A cloud of steam was rising from the soaked mattress.

'It broke,' I gasped.

Dad reached out and scooped me into his arms. We all but flew down the stairs with Petra at our heels and the rest of the family thumping along behind. In the kitchen he stood me in the ancient pot sink, put the plug in and turned on the cold tap. Then he turned to Mum. 'I'll take him, love. I'll get the car out. He needs to be down to casualty, fast as we can.'

I remember very little about that ride to town, which is a pity, because Dad told me afterwards that it was one of the hairiest he'd every taken. The snow was flying, the wind howling, and he had all on to keep the faithful Traveller on the road – which was covered in ice and more or less indistinguishable from the fields around us. But he got us there in one piece, and there to greet me was the nurse I'd fallen in love with on my last visit.

'Don't I know you?' she asked as she inspected my red and blistered foot.

'Yes,' I whispered.

'Ah, I remember now.' She'd spotted my big toe, where the new nail was still not fully grown. 'Tinned rice pudding, right?'

They smothered my foot with some kind of soothing cream, gave me something for the pain and put a light dressing over it. Then they let Dad carry me back to the car. By this time the snow had eased off, a snow-plough seemed to have been through, and the ride home was relatively uneventful.

I got two weeks off school, two weeks punctuated by a couple of return visits to casualty. Each time I asked the same question: 'Can I play outside yet?' I was missing out on sledging down the hill by the church, snowball fights and a monster slide my mates had created on the school playground. The answer was always the same. No.

By the time I got the green light, well, you can guess what. The weather had changed, the sun had returned and all that magical world of snow and ice had melted away.

Honk

When Dad and Mum decided that I could have a pet they had no idea what they were letting themselves in for. Come to think of it, neither did I.

As soon as we moved into Beech Farm House, animals were at the top of the agenda. Gillian and Christine, of course, wanted a horse. Make that horses. And they got them. There was Justine and Snap, Pippa and Shandy; and Solitaire; and Snap the Shetland pony. So my sisters were in seventh heaven – and, to be fair, I had my share of pleasure from them too. In return for mucking them out I could get a ride every so often – just so long as the girls weren't preparing for some event or other.

The thing was, they never let me forget that these were their horses, that the paddock and stables and the little exercise yard were their domain. They had all the gear – the riding breeches, the jackets, the hard hats. And I had … well, I had my jeans and wellies and a flat cap. Step out of line and I'd get a sharp reminder as to what Christine's riding-crop was for.

Not unnaturally, I wanted an animal of my own, and Mum and Dad both agreed it would only be fair. It wouldn't be a rabbit, or a guinea-pig, because the girls had got one of those each, as well the horses. Would it be another dog? A friend for Petra? A Jack Russell perhaps, always handy if there were rats around – which there were. Every autumn they'd start to wander in off the fields, looking for a cosy spot to see out the winter.

Mum suggested another cat, a friend for Purdy. She could certainly do with some help in the pest control department. Night after night we could hear scampering noises from under the floorboards. Purdy did her best, but she was getting on in years – unlike the mice, who seemed to be breeding like flies.

We did indeed get a pal for her, Rosie, a black cat with a strange habit. Of all the places available to her she decided that her favourite spot for a nap was behind the wheels of the car. How she escaped being squashed remained a mystery. Somehow she always seemed to slip away just as the car moved.

Rosie was all right, but she wasn't mine. She was another family pet. What I wanted was an animal I could call my own, preferably something exotic. There was a lad at school, for instance, who had an iguana. It looked fantastic – like a small dragon – but it wasn't exactly a thrill a minute: when I went to his house to look at it it just sat there waiting to be fed grasshoppers, which he bought by mail order. There was another youth who had a tarantula. That had a certain appeal: the girls hated spiders and it would be a handy weapon in the war that was constantly breaking out between us. But what else could you do with it? Not a lot, was my conclusion.

But when I saw one of the presenters on Blue Peter with a pet python I decided that that was just the thing for me. I went to the library and took out a book about reptiles. And another one. And then a few more. I pored over the pictures and read them cover to cover, then came down for breakfast one Saturday morning and announced to the family that that was what I was going to have. And before they could protest I started to list the python's many attributes.

'I mean, it doesn't eat much,' I said. 'It says in this book it can eat one small animal and it won't need anything else all week. And they hardly make any mess.'

'What sort of small animal are you talking about?' Mum asked, her cup of tea halfway to her mouth.

'Watch out girls, he'll be after your guinea-pigs.' Phil was choking on his Shredded Wheat.

Gillian shrieked, and Christine declared that the minute a snake appeared in the house she'd pack a bag and go to live with her friend in Easingwold. 'Or your rabbit,' Phil added, grinning at me as Christine aimed a kick at him under the table.

'Calm down, girls,' Mum said, before turning to me with her sternest face on. 'You will not be having a snake, Michael, and that's final.'

'But they're really useful,' I protested. 'I mean, crooks and so on – it said in this book that people who have pythons never get burgled. And if a burglar does get in, then the snake slithers around him and – you know, squeezes him to death. I could get a medal.'

'You're thinking of a boa constrictor,' Phil said. 'They're the ones that crush their victims. Like this.' And he put his hands around my neck and tightened his grip.

'Let your brother go,' Dad said, from behind his Daily Mail. 'Now.'

'I don't think we need discuss this any further,' Mum said. 'I'd no more think of leaving a snake on guard than – than a wolf.' She shuddered as she buttered her toast, 'And even if they are good guards it wouldn't be much consolation for you if I ended up in York District Hospital with a heart attack, would it? So let's just forget about it, Michael. If you want a pet you find something sensible. Something with four legs and a tail. Do you hear?'

'It's not fair,' I said, scowling at them all.

'Do you hear?'

'The girls have got horses. Why can't I have what I want?'

'Four legs and a tail,' Dad repeated. 'You heard what your mother said.'

I left the table and stormed out of the house, raging at the injustice of it all. The girls always got their way. Why wouldn't anyone listen to reason?

Once I was outside I started to calm down. The sun was shining, a warm breeze was blowing, and an old grey tractor was coming down the road pulling a cartload of straw bales. Seeing who it was perched on the seat and bouncing along with his pipe nodding up and down, I ran after him. I'd been hanging around Swales' farm in my spare time ever since we moved out to Crayke, and I'd got to know the farmer. Sometimes on a Saturday he'd give me odd jobs to do – sweeping up the yard, mucking out the cowshed and so on for a few coins. When Old Man Swales got out of the cab and saw me he beckoned me across the yard to a pen he'd set up in one corner.

Looking back, I doubt that he was much more than forty-five years old, but he had the portly outline of a prosperous farmer, his hair was going grey, he smoked a pipe with a curved stem and he always carried a stick, limping a bit as he walked – the result, he liked to say, of an argument with a bull, which he lost. To us lads he seemed absolutely ancient, and Old Man Swales he was.

He leaned on the horizontal scaffold-pole that formed the top rung of the enclosure, nodded at me and took his pipe from his mouth. He pointed into the pen. 'What d'you reckon, lad?' Inside was a fat sow lying on her side while a swarm of little pink piglets scrambled over each other, looking for the best source of milk.

At first I didn't say anything. A thought had occurred to me, and I couldn't resist sharing it. 'A piglet,' I said, 'a piglet has four legs and a tail.'

Old Man Swales grunted, puffed on his pipe and said, 'You're a bright lad, young Michael, and don't let anyone tell you otherwise. Them little pigs are indeed quadrupeds.'

'Aye. I've always wanted one of them,' I said. 'You know, a piglet.'

'Is that so?' Mister Swales puffed on his pipe. Otherwise there was no response. I looked at the piglets and started counting out loud. 'Eight … ten … twelve …' That's when I had the brainwave. Not just any old brainwave, but the best brainwave I'd had since I pulled the weathervane stunt. I carefully counted the litter once more. 'That's bad luck, that,' I said, pointing at the piglets.

He frowned. 'I don't follow you, lad. They all look healthy enough to me. What are you getting at?'

I didn't answer at once, I was busy re-counting them. Then I said, 'Having thirteen in the litter. Thirteen's unlucky, isn't it? Maybe you should ... you know, give one away.'

At that Old Man Swales leaned back and laughed so hard that he let his pipe drop to the ground. He picked it up, wiped the stem on his trousers and popped it back in his mouth. Then he looked into the pen. Most of the litter were sucking away, their little legs scrabbling for a foothold, but there was one, a bit smaller than the rest, which was running up and down looking for a free teat – and not finding one. Old Man Swales stepped over the railing, grabbed hold of it in one broad hand, and passed it to me.

'Go on, lad. That's for your cheek. But you'll have to look after it, mind. It's only a little runt of a thing.'

At first I was lost for words. He'd called my bluff. I stood there as the little porker wriggled around in my arms, pressing his snout into my stomach and looking for – well, I soon realised what he was after.

'What do I do?' I asked, looking down at the piglet, which had already clamped his jaws around my T-shirt and was sucking in more and more of it.

Old Man Swales' jowls quivered. 'That's for you to decide,' he chuckled. 'She's all yours now, lad.'

'She?' It hadn't occurred to me to think about boy piglets and girl piglets, but now that I knew I'd got a little sow I couldn't help wishing I'd picked a hog.

Farmer Swales had stopped laughing and was looking serious. 'Right,' he said, 'you want to tek her home quick as you can, find her a nice warm bed and' – he paused and asked, 'any baby brothers or sisters in your house?'

I shook my head and grunted as the piglet wriggled around in my arms and did a little poo down my trousers.

'Hm.' He took his pipe from his mouth and looked me up and down. 'You'd best ask your mother. See if she's got one of them feeding bottles wi' a – ' He checked himself once more. 'Tell you what, I reckon I might have a spare. Follow me, lad.' With that he tapped his pipe on the wall of the pen and set off to the back door of the farmhouse. I followed, struggling to keep hold of my new pet.

In the kitchen was a big wooden table, and on the table was a big old roasting dish, and in the roasting dish was a plump hen. He lifted her out and took her to the door. 'I've told this bugger before. You live outside!' he shouted. 'Go on wi' you!' Then he picked two eggs from the tin. 'Here, you may as well put them in your pocket,' he said, handing them to me. But I had my hands full, so he put them back where he found them.

Then he opened a drawer, pulled out a baby's feeding-bottle and handed it to me.

'Here's what you need, lad.' Just keep her fed with lots of warm milk and she'll be fine.' He took a last look at her and nodded. 'Aye, you feed her up and she'll soon have some meat on her bones.'

I hurried home, trying to think of a suitable name. Piglet? No. Percy? Not that either. Maybe Fatty? No, that wouldn't be kind.

Back at the house everybody was still in the kitchen, the girls helping Mum with the dishes, Dad measuring a length of copper pipe, and Phil standing by the back door polishing his shoes. I brushed past him. Mum looked up from the sink. The plate she was holding plopped back into the washing-up bowl.

'Michael Richard Pannett.'

'Yes, Mum?'

'What is that you are holding in your hands?'

'Whatever it is it doesn't half honk,' Phil said, holding his nose.

I looked down at the piglet, who had nuzzled her snout into the crook of my arm and fallen asleep. 'This is … Honk,' I said. 'She's a baby pig and she's called Honk.'

'Where on earth did you get her from – and what is that mess down those clean trousers I put out for you this morning?'

'Mr Swales gave her to me. He had thirteen, you see, and that's unlucky, and I said I wanted a pet and it had to have four legs and a tail, and he said – '

'You are not having a pig as a pet, do you hear me?'

Before I could protest, Christine joined in. 'You can't be having a nasty stinky pig as a pet,' she said, screwing up her face.

'Great fat ugly things,' said Gillian.

'All that rolling around in the mud,' Christine added.

I wasn't having that. I came back at them, all guns blazing. 'You shut up,' I said. 'They're only mucky if you let 'em get mucky. And they're as intelligent as – as … '

Christine was laughing. 'Yeah, as what?'

'As you for a start. And anyway, they're more use than a stupid old horse.'

'Oh they are, are they?'

'Aye, 'cos at least when it gets big and fat you can …'

'You can what?'

That's where Dad stepped in. 'You know, Michael has a point.' Everyone was silent. They usually were when Dad spoke. 'Give the boy his due,' he said. 'We did stipulate four legs and a tail.'

Mum sighed and rolled her eyes. She was about to lose the argument, and she knew it. Dad looked at me and said, 'If you're willing to look after the pig – and I mean every day, rain or shine, not just when you feel like it – if you're willing to take it seriously, you can have one, so long as you understand …'

He paused. I knew what was coming – or thought I did, but I never expected Dad, of all people, to gloss over it. 'So long as you understand that you don't keep a pig forever.' He gave me a meaningful look and left it at that.

'Well, just because your father says you can keep it, doesn't mean you can keep it in the house,' Mum said. 'Come on, outside with you – and I'll have those trousers off you if you don't mind.'

I took Honk outside and Dad followed me.

'This way,' he said, and led me to one of the disused outhouses that adjoined his workshop. 'She can live in here to start with. Then we'll have to build her a proper pen. A sty, I should say. A proper little pig-sty.'

We put down some clean straw, found an old enamelled baking tin and filled it with water, then laid Honk in her bed.

'She'll be hungry,' I said. 'Old Man Sw–, Mister Swales I mean, gave me a bottle, look.' I took it out of my pocket.

'Well, go and fill it up then,' Dad said.

Honk was already waking up and trying to get to her feet. I ran to the house, went to the refrigerator and filled the bottle, then dashed back. She wasn't having it at first – even when I squeezed the milk out of the teat and into her mouth.

'She doesn't like it,' I said. We were both crouched down beside the little crib we'd rigged up.

'No, she won't,' Dad said. He reached out and felt the bottle, then got to his feet. 'I'll be back in a minute.'

When he returned the bottle was warm. 'Dunked it in a bowl of hot water,' he said. 'Cold milk's not good for them. They want it at body temperature. That's how it comes from their mother.' He prodded the piglet's snout with the rubber teat. She opened her mouth and started sucking. 'I've put a bit of sugar in too. See, she's loving it now.'

She certainly was. From then on, the only problem we had in feeding her was in finding enough to satisfy her amazing appetite. She simply loved eating.

Getting her to love her new home, however, was a different matter. I spent the rest of the day with her, arranging and re-arranging the bedding, building a miniature pen of old bricks around her, and pestering Dad for a sheet of plywood to make a lid. At midday I took my sandwich out to eat with her, but when it came to teatime and Mum's announcement that it was a special treat, fishfingers, I tucked her into her bed of straw, gave her one last feed and made my way to the back door. As I arrived there and kicked off my wellies, there was Honk, right beside me, nosing her way inside.

Mum was standing in the doorway trying to block her path. She might as well have been a York City defender trying to impede Johann Cruyff's progress into the penalty area. Honk skipped past her and trotted across the kitchen with her little pink snout in the air, pausing every so often to sniff the air.

Mum turned and looked at her, then sighed and said, 'Well, I have to admit it. She's very cute, isn't she?'

And from that day on, until she was almost fully grown, Honk was a house pig, a true domestic pet. The theory was that she lived in the outhouse; the reality was that she spent her days around the kitchen – when she wasn't sunning herself on the back step, that is. Feeding her and mucking out was up to me, but all of us shared the responsibility for making sure that the door that led into the rest of the house was kept firmly closed. We were good at that – at first. We were, to use Dad's word, vigilant. We had to be. We knew full well that if we let her escape there would be trouble. Big trouble.

I think it was a school day. In fact, I'm sure it was. I remember rushing home, bursting through the back door, grabbing a couple of ginger nuts and making a mad dash for the living room. Not only was there the usual competition for a seat on the sofa, rather than the floor, but today was Mister Benn, one of my favourite programmes, and I was determined to watch it in comfort. I hadn't been sitting there for more than a few minutes when I felt a cool moist snout nuzzling my bare leg. Honk had grown at an amazing rate over the previous few weeks. She was now on a solid diet and was about the same size as Petra, only much fatter.

'Good girl,' I said, and carried on gazing at the screen while Honk nosed around me.

Once she realised that I'd nothing more than the biscuit-crumbs from my lap to offer her she snuggled down next to Petra, and the pair of them were soon snoring in perfect harmony.

'Michael!'

Turning around, I saw Mum at the door. She had a frying pan in one hand and a wooden spoon in the other, and she looked very, very cross. Beside me, I could feel Honk wriggling as she nestled between my leg and Petra's haunch.

'What did we agree about that animal?'

Whoops, I thought.

'Michael, I'm waiting for an answer.'

'Er – we agreed that she wasn't to …' Honk was awake now, quivering slightly, as if she too felt the fear. 'Did someone leave the door open?'

'Yes, Michael, they most certainly did. And would I be right in thinking that somebody might have been Michael Richard Pannett?'

There was no point denying it, not with Mum in that mood. On the other hand, there was no harm in trying.

'It was Gillian,' I said.

Gillian didn't hear my accusation. She'd taken advantage of the interruption to change channels and was already glued to her beloved Clangers.

Mum strode towards me. I could feel the rickety old floorboards shake under her angry tread, but mostly I was focused on the frying-pan, which she held at shoulder height.

'When I tell you that that animal is not allowed beyond the kitchen, I mean it. Do you hear me?'

I could hear her okay, and so could Honk. If Mum had unnerved me, she'd panicked the poor little piglet. Honk relieved herself – half on the rug, the rest on Petra – and shot off into the hallway.

'Now look what you've done,' I said.

'Never mind that. Get after it!' Mum shouted. 'If that little … thing gets into the bedrooms there'll be no pocket money for you until – until …'

I didn't wait for her to select a random date. Whatever she decided on wasn't going to be good news for me. I set off into the hallway and galloped up the stairs just as Honk's plump bottom slid around the corner of the landing and out of sight. I had no trouble plotting her course, however: she'd laid a trail of evidence at intervals of about six feet – all the way to Mum and Dad's bedroom door, which was wide open.

It hardly needs saying that I was getting into more trouble by the minute. After I'd caught Honk and persuaded her back down the stairs I was given a shovel, a mop, a bucket and a bottle of disinfectant – but no instructions as to how much to use. Looking back, I can only imagine that I overdid it. I got rid of all the mess, but the sickly smell of piggy-poo was replaced by an overpowering stench of Dettol, which lingered for days and days and days. On top of all that there was, as I feared, no pocket money for four weeks.

Honk now lived outside, permanently. And, being almost full-grown, she had a proper sty, which Dad built of breeze-blocks. It had a stout wooden gate and a little sort of house she could sleep in. Then the day came, as we knew, deep down, that it must, when she stopped gaining in weight. Not that we were weighing her, of course. It was Old Man Swales who pointed it out when he came by to drop off some spuds that Mum had ordered.

'Now then, lad.' He feigned to hand me the fifty-six-pound sack, and laughed as I tried to grab it and, naturally enough, staggered back under its weight. 'How's that little runty thing I gave you?'

'She's over here,' I said, and led the way to the sty at the bottom of the yard. Dad came out of his workshop and joined us.

Old Man Swales peered over the wall. Honk was on her feet attacking a couple of huge swedes we'd put in for her. 'By heck,' he said, 'she's grown.' Then he turned to Dad. 'Tell you the truth, Jeff, I never expected her to last.' And with that he patted me on the head. 'You've done a wonderful job, lad. I hope you Mum and Dad go halves wi' you when they ship her off to market.'

'Market?' I didn't like the sound of that, at all.

Old Man Swales looked at Dad, and raised his eyebrows. Dad looked at me. 'Well yes,' he said, 'I think we agreed that she wouldn't be around forever. That was part of the agreement, remember?'

I don't know whether I was a tough kid, or an unfeeling one. I remember the day, not much later – it was a Saturday – when Dad borrowed a trailer from Mr Swales and took her to the abattoir. Over the next week or two I saw the weeds start to sprout around the edge of her little run, and then one day Dad helped me shovel it clean and hose it down.

Some time after that we sat down to Sunday dinner and there on the table were two roasting dishes. On one was a piece of beef, on the other a huge leg of pork all covered in crackling. I remember Phil sitting down and going, 'Wow! Look at that', and Mum explaining that she and the girls were eating the beef, and it was up to us three to decide whether we really wanted to eat meat from a pig who not so long ago had been a household pet.

I looked at Dad, who shrugged his shoulders and said, 'Well, we gave Honk a better life than she would've had if she'd been raised on the farm, so speaking for myself …'

And that was that. He carved, and we three tucked in.

Grandpa

When Dad explained that we could afford to move out to Crayke because of his promotion, he could have added that the move was in part due to Grandpa.

Whenever I think of Grandpa I think of the Blacksmiths Arms in Huntington. It was run by a fellow they called Smudge. Maybe he was a Smith, but I can't be certain.

Before we made the move out to Crayke I spent a lot of time there – sitting outside, of course, with a bottle of pop and a bag of crisps. In those days a child wasn't welcomed in a pub. You might go to the door and peek inside, but all you'd get was a view of a row of men at the bar with their backs to you, maybe a few more at a table – one of whom would be sure to turn around and tell you to clear off. Sometimes a kid's mother might send him down to get his Dad home for Sunday lunch – and the mere sight of his youngster at the door would generally have the embarrassed fellow downing his pint and getting out as fast as he could while his mates took the mickey. But, as a rule, in those days the pub was for adults only.

Sometimes my mates and I would go down there to see whether we could find a discarded beer or pop bottle, which we'd take to the shop to reclaim the deposit. We'd rummage through the waste bins too and maybe add to our collection. The return wasn't much – something like two or three pence per bottle, as I recall – but on a good day you'd gather up enough empties to treat yourself to a tube of Smarties or, if you'd done really well, an ice-cream cone with a chocolate flake in it.

However, when Grandpa retired he felt he deserved to enjoy a simple pleasure that had been denied him through his working life. Around midday he'd take a stroll across the fields and enjoy a refreshing pint – and when I was off school he'd let me go with him. If it was a fine day he might sit outside with me, but more often than not he'd leave me on my own, with instructions not to talk to any strangers. I didn't mind. I had my treats, and maybe a comic to read, and after half an hour or so we'd walk back across the fields.

Sometimes, on the road, we'd see a lorry go by and he'd wave at the driver and say, 'Aye, he's a good lad. I took him on, back in 1958.'

Grandpa had been a transport manager at Terry's chocolate factory in York, one of a number of my family who worked there. My Aunt June, who used to visit every other week and come to stay when we were at Crayke, she'd been personal assistant to Sir Peter Terry himself, and used to bring us home lots of goodies at Christmas and Easter. Like most of their employees, she was very proud of their chocolate, and would tell anybody who cared to listen that it was superior to any of Rowntrees' products.

In the pub Grandpa drank Guinness. I only knew that because he told me. He said that when I grew up that's what I should drink. He said that he owed his long and healthy life to the two pints he'd have on those lunchtime outings.

Like a lot of older people, Grandpa liked to talk about the past – about steam trains, about horse-drawn days and about how cheap everything used to be when he was a lad.

But one thing he never talked about – and I always wished he would – was the war. Either war, because he served in both. Like most boys, I wanted to hear about guns and bombs and tanks and fighting from someone who'd actually been there. War was still very much on our minds, and to us lads it all seemed very exciting. When we weren't playing cowboys and Indians we were pretending to be American soldiers, or British fighter-pilots. We'd act out scenes we'd seen in the old black-and-white films that came on television, sometimes things we'd read about in our comics. I knew that I was seeing exaggerated versions of the real thing, and was dying to ask Grandpa what it was really like to be at war, but Mum had warned me, many times.

'Don't you ever ask him,' she'd say. 'He'd rather forget all about it. He had a terrible time in the trenches.' And then she'd add, 'He was a very brave man, your grandfather.'

She told me that he had medals – seven of them – tucked away in the box he kept on his mantelpiece.

For years I wondered what they looked like – and what he won them for – but it was never discussed. The little wooden box, lovingly polished, went with him when he entered a care home and took pride of place on his bedside table. We used to visit him, and I always looked at it and wondered, what was the story behind them? As he aged, his mind started to go. It was desperately sad to see, and quite disturbing. I remember the time I went to visit him and he got it into his head that I was a German. I must have grown taller, and with his failing eyesight I suppose he could've mistaken me for a grown-up. One minute he was standing up to greet me, the next he had his hands around my throat and it was as if he was trying to strangle me. I think one of the staff stepped in to defuse the situation, but I remained shocked that such a kind and gentle man could seem so determined to do me damage.

It was only after he died that we were allowed to look at the medals and learn that one of them was awarded for bravery in the field. We'd been to his funeral and brought a few of the relatives back to the house for tea and sandwiches. Everybody was talking about Grandpa and that seemed to prompt Mum to tell us what she knew of his days in uniform.

In the Great War, as she called it, he joined a cavalry regiment. He'd grown up with working horses, so it seemed the obvious place for him to serve. His job was to ride a horse that was one of a team pulling heavy guns through the mud. He didn't like the work and felt for the poor animals, having to work so hard in awful conditions, sometimes under bombardment from enemy artillery. At times he'd end up on the front line, hiding in a trench as a barrage opened up. It was in the trenches, Mum told us, that he earned his medal for bravery.

'The way he told it – and he only ever told it once in my hearing – he and his companions were dug in opposite the German lines. They were so close that they could see and hear each other. They actually shouted insults to and fro when there was nothing going on, or sang songs, trying to drown each other out. This one time one of the Germans threw a hand grenade which landed in your Grandpa's trench, right beside him. He rushed forward and picked it up.'

'What did he do that for?' I asked.

'So that he could throw it back at them – or at least into No Man's Land.'

'But wasn't he scared it'd go off?'

'I should think he was. But he acted without thinking. He always said that that's how a lot of medals were won – fellows just doing daft things without thinking. If they died, that was that; but if they survived they were heroes. What he did that day saved several lives, or at least a lot of horrible injuries. As it happened, it did explode, just as he released it.'

'Wow. So was he injured?'

'Blinded, and sent to a field hospital.'

'So that makes Grandpa a real hero,' I said.

Mum shook her head. 'He never called himself a hero, and we shouldn't either. He always insisted that the heroes were the ones who died. He hated the war. Thought it was a terrible business, and that's why he never talked about it again. Imagine if you'd seen your friends blown to pieces and had to come home without them.'

I tried, but I found it hard. Still, at the very least it was good to hear a little about Grandpa's wartime experiences. He may not have liked the word 'hero' but now that I knew what had happened I felt very proud of him.

'So what did he do in the Second World War?' I asked. 'Did he go back and join the cavalry again?'

Mum smiled. 'No,' she said. 'There hardly was any cavalry by then. It was nearly all cars and trucks. Besides, he was a married man, too old for normal service. He joined what they call the Home Guard – like Dad's Army on the television. They had a base at Poppleton. Every night after work he'd hop on his bike and pedal out there to do whatever they did. Training, I suppose. In case we were invaded.'

I thought for a moment, then said, 'How come he can see okay when he got blinded by that grenade?'

'Oh, that was just temporary. Whatever they did to him in the hospital they cured him, and he went back into the line with his horses.

Mum and Dad inherited some money from Grandpa's will. I don't know how much, but it was a substantial amount. And, as I said, it helped them with the move out to Crayke.

As well as that, they sat down and talked about what little luxury they might allow themselves out of the windfall, and decided on a piano. They bought a secondhand upright. None of us could play, but Dad decided he wanted to give it a try. Typically, he didn't bother with a teacher, just bought a book and sat down and taught himself. That's the kind of man he was, and he very quickly learnt to play like a professional. Mum was ever so impressed and would constantly praise him – something I don't think he objected to.

There was a down-side to the piano, unfortunately. It turned out that there was enough money in Grandpa's bequest for us children to have lessons. Christine hardly needed them: she was a natural like Dad. I wasn't. I had no desire to play the thing, but every week we had to walk to the house of a Mrs Cundall. She was what you'd call old school: ruled by the metronome, and not prepared to take any nonsense from a fidgety little boy. It was all about sitting up straight at the piano – 'and keep those wrists in position, Michael!' Every time I let them drop I got an old-fashioned reminder, much as you'd dish out to a recalcitrant horse, except that the skin on my forearms was a lot thinner than a horse's.

Much as I cherished my memories of Grandpa, and much as I respected him for his deeds in the war, I often used to wish he'd spent all his money before he died. But I never said that. It would've seemed ungrateful – and besides, Mrs Cundall sacked me in the end. She came to the same conclusion I'd come to the very first time we met: I was never going to be a pianist.

Girls

'Girls.' Phil said, 'Take it from me, they're nothing but trouble.'

That was pretty ripe, coming from a lad who had a string of girl-friends, and who spent half his spare time in front of the mirror trying to get his hair to behave – or squeezing his spots.

I remember wondering why he was so bothered about spots. Being eleven years old, and not yet afflicted by acne, I thought they were cool, a sure sign that you were now a man. While he peered into the glass, alternately squeezing and applying dollops of Clearasil, I stood on tiptoes and peered over his shoulder, studying my face, hoping to find a single blackhead I could call my own.

There's no doubt about it: having an older brother is a blessing and a curse. You have this idea that they know everything worth knowing, so you pester them, and they tell you things you're probably too young to hear. Then, when you wind up in trouble, they laugh. I was always trying to worm secrets out of Phil, right up until the time he left home.

The day would come when I'd tag along with him and try to get served in the Durham Ox, but that was well in the future. At ten and eleven, it was his knowledge of the fair sex that intrigued me. At least, the knowledge he professed to have. To me, he seemed a real man of the world, and I hung on his every word.

I don't know when I started taking an interest in girls, but I can say with confidence that it was a very long time ago. In fact, now that I think about it I'm struggling to remember a time when I wasn't getting distracted by them. My first week at school I came home and told my Mum that the little lass who sat next to me at the dinner table had shiny hair, that she wore a kilt, was very pretty, and that she was my girlfriend.

'Yes, dear,' she said. 'Now run along and play, will you?'

As my first Christmas at school drew near, I sat at the kitchen table and made a card for our form teacher, Miss Dalton. Mum watched with interest, and helped me write my name in block letters, but when I put a row of Xs underneath she made me rub them out.

'Suppose everybody in the class did that,' she said. 'Poor Miss Dalton, she'd be smothered.'

Next day, before assembly, I borrowed a red crayon, scrawled a big red X on the card, and placed it on Miss Dalton's desk. I was in love with her, and I thought it only right that she should know.

On average, I fell in love about three times a term, and had my heart broken accordingly. For some reason, the girls just weren't as keen on me as I was on them. When I tried to chat them up they laughed at me and carried on playing with their skipping ropes and dolls. They seemed to enjoy being chased across the playground – if their shrieks were anything to go by – but whenever you caught one she'd stalk off to her friends and pretend to be outraged. Undaunted, I continued to chase them. And from time to time I did manage to get chatting – not that I really knew what to say. I just knew that I liked being in their company.

By the time I was in the top class of primary school I was confidently telling people that Julie and I were going out together. I even told Phil when he came up to bed one night. I thought I would impress him. I immediately wished I hadn't bothered.

'Oh aye,' he said, 'so this lass you're going out with. Where you taking her then?'

It was a fair question, to which I had no answer. To tell the truth, I hadn't really thought about what a date consisted of. I chewed it over for a moment or two and said, 'It's a secret. I promised not to tell.'

'Gonna take her fishing, are you?' he taunted me. ''Cos you can't afford to go to the flicks, can you? Eh? Not like me and my girl.'

Phil had a paper round. Every Saturday he got paid in cash. He loved to jingle all the coins in his pocket or, as now, spread them out on the bed and count them.

'As a matter of fact,' he said, 'you could say we're off on a fishing trip tomorrow night.'

I didn't speak. It had never occurred to me that you might take a girl fishing. Especially in the dark. It all sounded very grown-up, if not sinister.

Phil laughed as he scooped up his cash, put it into his pocket and stood up.

'Yep, we're off to see Jaws. The scariest film ever made. It's about a man-eating shark. I'll tell you all about it when we get home.' He looked down at me. 'Or maybe not. Don't want you getting night-mares. Anyway,' he said, 'take it from me. You should leave the girls alone. You'll only get into trouble.'

I really hated the way my big brother talked down to me as if he knew everything, but it would take more than a bit of sarcasm from him to put me off chasing girls. In fact, my interest intensified year by year – and I soon discovered that Phil was right about one thing. Girls could spell trouble, even when they didn't mean to. The trouble with Jackie started, strangely enough, with a fishing trip. And it would lead me to the place that so many of my early misadventures took me.

It was a gorgeous sunny day in late July. I'd just completed my final year in primary school. We'd put on our end-of-year show, said good-bye to our friends – and one or two enemies – and our teacher had wished us all good luck for the future. Yes, the future. Senior school. We were all worried about that, although none of us dared to admit it.

In any case, right now, with the whole of the summer holidays stretching ahead of us, it seemed a long way in the future. Six whole weeks away. And when you're eleven years old, six weeks can seem like a very long time indeed. Besides, I was never a great worrier. Let tomorrow look after itself, that's my motto. And in the meantime, live for the present.

I'd been to town the previous Saturday and bought a new fishing rod, and I couldn't wait to try it out. I called on my mate Simon. He liked to fish as well, and we agreed to go down to the River Foss together, to a little spot we knew of just the other side of Stillington. Simon had a big brother too, and it was he who had shown us this little hideaway.

So there we were, cycling through the village, free-wheeling down the hill, our back-packs bulging with supplies. We had sandwiches, crisps, a bottle of pop apiece, an assortment of sweets, and all our gear: hooks, bait, spare line, a net.

The entire day was at our disposal. The only constraint on our time was that we had to be back for tea. Neither of us had a watch, but of course in those days you didn't need one. Maybe it was our stomachs, maybe it was some sixth sense we inherited from our ancestors, but something always seemed to alert us to the fact that it was time to head for home – and somehow we always seemed to arrive just in time to be greeted by the smell of food cooking.

Home time, however, was far from my mind as I raced Simon through the village that morning, steering my bike with one hand, clasping my new rod under my free arm, the wind blowing through my hair. He'd got a head start on me, but I soon overtook him, almost nudging his shoulder. As he wobbled onto the verge and slammed on his brakes, I laughed aloud. I didn't have a care in the world.

Then I saw her.

Jackie was a year older than me and already in senior school. The rumour was that there were lads in the village aged fourteen and fifteen who'd asked her out. I'd just admired her from afar. But once – and how could I forget it? – once, when I was singing in the choir, I caught her eye and smiled at her. And she smiled back – in fact, I could've sworn she winked at me.

Now here she was in her flared purple trousers, her cheesecloth blouse and sporting a pair of sun-glasses with small, oval lenses. With her long blonde hair she looked like a film-star. She was walking towards me, a vision of loveliness. And she seemed to be waving at me.

Ask any bloke. It only takes a flicker of the hand, the hint of a smile, and your judgement and good sense go right out of the window. I leaned back on my saddle, took my left hand off the handlebar and waved back at her – with my brand-new fibre-glass rod. I was just drawing level with her as I hit the pothole. My rod slipped from my grasp, arrowed forward and went straight through the front wheel.

I've heard all sorts of things about what goes through people's minds when they have accidents. They see their life pass before their eyes. Everything goes slow-motion. They watch themselves as if they're in a film.

All I remember was seeing Jackie flapping her hand about once more, just as I took flight over the handlebars, and realising as I somersaulted through the air that she wasn't trying to attract my attention at all, but was trying to bat a wasp away from her face.

I was sprawled on my front. My bike lay in the road nearby, the rear wheel spinning. I could taste blood.

'You all right?' I rolled over and saw Simon standing over me, panting. I didn't answer.

Beside him stood the divine Jackie, leaning forward so that her hair fell forward and caressed my cheek. She'd taken off her sunglasses and was staring at my face, puckering up her lips as if she'd just bitten into a sour apple. I shaped my mouth to speak to her, and that's when I realised that bits of my front teeth were scattered around in my mouth. Whatever it was I was trying to say came out as a blur of mumbled syllables laced with a lot of bloody saliva.

Seeing me rise to my feet and pick up my bike, Jackie put her sunglasses back on and resumed her progress through the village. Simon helped me home, and Mum arranged a taxi to take me to casualty, where they put a couple of stitches in my lower lip and packed me off to the dentist.

That night, when Phil got back from town, he looked at my stitches and asked me what had happened. He laughed when I told him.

'See what I mean?' he said. 'Girls. They're nothing but trouble.'

Animal Farm

Living in a house with acres of land around us presented Mum and Dad with an unforeseen problem: how to say 'no' when we told them that, as well as the cat, the dog and the horses, we wanted geese, and ducks and hens. And while we're at it, how about a few guinea-fowl?

They'd seen the girls knuckle down to looking after the horses; they'd seen me mucking out Honk's pen, day after day until her demise, so they knew we were up to it.

Neither could they say, as they had at the old house, 'But where will you put them all?' There was more land out there than anybody knew what to do with. On a foggy day you couldn't see the far end of it. There was space for cricket, and football, and the horses, and any amount of livestock.

So the invasion – and the fun – began.

It started with the guinea-fowl, George and Mildred – two plump birds with pea-sized heads and even smaller brains, or so we thought. The names suited them: just like the characters in the TV sitcom they were raucously loud, and always seemed to be arguing with each other or with any other creature – animal or human – that was foolish enough to approach them. Petra certainly gave these new arrivals a wide berth.

Having said that, they were easy enough to look after, once we'd given up trying to control their movements. The trick, we discovered, was to leave well alone. If they wanted to spend the day looking for bugs in the long grass down the orchard, fine. If they decided to spend the day on the roof, clinging to the ridge tiles as the wind tugged at their silver-grey feathers, so be it. It was their choice. If they wanted to set off down the middle of the road, dodging the traffic as they pecked around for bits of spilled corn – well, it was their lives on the white line. They were, quite simply, cussed. Try to persuade them to go somewhere that would suit them better and they'd head in the opposite direction.

Just think about trying to grab them and they'd be off, not so much running as sprinting. These birds were lightning-fast. If, by some miracle, you did manage to get your hands around them they'd slip away and fly up a nearby tree. They liked trees, particularly the old ash down at the far end of the garden, and would spend long hours up there, doubtless laughing at us as we searched for them in all the obvious places.

The only time you could guarantee to find them was when it got dark. To start with, every evening as the light faded we'd scour the yard and the fields, trying to find them and nearly always failing. Then, when we went to lock up the hens, there they'd be, back in the little pen we'd made for them and settling down for the night. They seemed to look at you as if to say, what was all that fuss about? Here we are.

People used to ask us why we kept them when they seemed so much trouble, and all we could do was shrug and say, 'Well, look at them.'

There was no denying the fact: they were very pretty birds. When they wandered out onto the road, passing motorists would slow down to gaze at them. Some would even get out and photograph them. More than once we had a knock at the door and found some stranger asking if there was any chance of us raising chicks. The answer to that was always 'no'. For some reason Mildred never seemed to lay any eggs – at least, not where we could find them.

But Mildred's failings in that department didn't bother us. We had a flock of hens of various shapes and sizes – all of them named – and one proud cockerel who strutted about like some Arab potentate with his own personal harem. His feathers were a splendid mixture of gold, brown and black, topped by a bright red comb. We were never quite sure what breed he was but after some discussion we came to the conclusion that he must be a Rhode Island Red.

Once our little flock had settled in they started laying ... and laying, and laying. And every time we went to collect the eggs the cockerel felt it was his duty to attack us, making a dive for our ankles with his beak. The only way to distract him was to go in with a bit of feed in a bucket. You could generally rely on his appetite overcoming his instinct for protecting his flock.

We fed them a mixture of household scraps and proper layers' mash that Dad brought home from town in large paper sacks. Towards evening time we scattered a few handfuls of corn around the run so that the birds would fill their crops before settling down. From time to time Dad told us to scatter a bit of grit, which they needed to break down the corn.

We kept a bucket in the kitchen for potato peelings, cabbage trimmings, leftovers and the like, and every morning we had to mix the contents with enough dry feed and water to fill the six-foot length of cast-iron guttering that served as a feeding trough. The rule was to go out first thing, fill the trough, then open the henhouse door and retreat. We learned the hard way that standing in the way of a stroppy cockerel with vicious spurs and fourteen hungry hens with sharp beaks was asking for trouble.

Not surprisingly, there were mornings when you'd wake up, bleary-eyed, and go through the routine on auto-pilot. That's when mistakes occurred.

Just my luck that my turn fell on a wild and windy morning when the rain was lashing down. It was the first day of a new school term. I rolled out of bed, put on the new school trousers that Mum had bought me, threw my dressing gown on and stumbled downstairs. In the kitchen I grabbed the bucket of leftovers. It was an unappetising mess: in amongst it I could identify a tangle of leftover spaghetti, some lumpy custard and the remains of a boiled beetroot. You lucky birds, I thought, as I stirred in the layers' mash and topped it up with warm water. Then I stepped into my school shoes, also brand new, and opened the kitchen door.

Outside, and still not fully awake, I went down the yard, entered the run and opened the door of the henhouse. Out they all trotted, with the cockerel in the lead, swarming around my legs as I approached the trough.

As I poured out the contents of the pail I realised my mistake. The birds were all scrabbling over my feet or perched on the edge of the trough; some were in it, and, as I tilted the bucket, one of them managed to get inside. I turned the pail upside-down. Out came the bird, covered in food, the others clambering over her to get at the slimy gobs of custard that hung from her bedraggled feathers. The cockerel, meanwhile, had grabbed one end of a piece of spaghetti and was tugging at it. A big black hen had hold of the other end, and they settled down to a tug-of-war.

Meanwhile two other hens had discovered the custard and were wading through it, picking out the lumps, which they then shook, splattering my clean trousers and polished shoes with dollops of yellow matter flecked purple with beetroot juice.

Back at the house I got no sympathy at all, just gales of laughter from the girls and a stern rebuke from Mum.

'Michael Richard Pannett, what have you done to those nice new trousers I put out for you? And ... just look at those shoes. Really! Is there any point in my trying?'

It wasn't all trouble, having the hens. There were, of course, the eggs – once we devised a safe way of collecting them. When it became apparent just how aggressive the cockerel was, Dad built an extension to the henhouse, a whole row of nesting boxes which could be opened from the outside. That way we didn't have to disturb them – or the cockerel. Lifting a plump warm hen off a bed of clean straw and finding a couple of pale brown eggs under her is one of those pleasures, like home-baked bread, fresh from the oven, that you never tire of – and never forget.

Sadly, it wasn't always that simple. Most of the year the chickens ran free, and that meant that they'd occasionally go missing. It's only natural for a hen to try to hatch out her eggs and raise a brood of youngsters, and they soon worked out that that wasn't going to happen if they kept laying in the boxes. Every now and then we'd find one of them under a hedge, sitting on half a dozen eggs.

Sometimes one would disappear, then show up a week or two later with half a dozen fluffy little chicks around her ankles. We kids were enchanted, of course, but Dad used to stroke his chin and stare at them. We soon learned what was on his mind. As they grew, which they did rapidly, he'd stare a bit more, and before long he'd be able to distinguish those that were hen birds from those that weren't. Those that weren't were allowed to grow to a certain size, then ended up on the dining table.

Looking back, I suppose we must have saved ourselves a lot of money with all this livestock. And we made a bit too, selling eggs on the roadside, along with the excess produce from Dad's vegetable garden and greenhouse. Customers put their money in a big round biscuit tin, the honesty box, and we'd collect it every night.

Dad spent a lot of time down the garden, or in his glasshouse. If I couldn't find him in his workshop and wanted to speak to him, it was a fair bet that's where he'd be, surrounded by pots and seed packets, sometimes sneaking a crafty cigarette when he thought nobody was about.

As far as Mum and the rest of us were concerned he'd given up smoking, and to be fair we never saw him doing it around the house. But he must have found it hard, especially as nearly everybody else smoked in those days. I don't think he ever fooled Mum, however: it was just a case of 'out of sight and out of mind'.

I think Dad's dream would have been complete self-sufficiency. He took enormous pride in sitting down to a Christmas dinner of home-produced food. The spuds, the parsnips, the sprouts, carrots and leeks would all be home-grown, and the goose most years. With the help of a little paraffin heater he'd even manage to produce a few lettuces in midwinter, and every year when his tomato harvest was over he'd put the last few green ones in a drawer, wrapped in newspaper. Then he'd pull them out, red and shiny, and serve them up in one of the best china bowls for our Boxing Day tea.

Mum was well pleased with all this free produce. Apart from the business with Honk, there was only one thing they disagreed over, and that was the geese that arrived one day. They were noisy and they were aggressive, she complained. Just the job, Dad liked to say, for keeping any intruders away – and then he'd remind us that our Roman ancestors had used them as guards.

These geese didn't let us down. As soon as a visitor or a delivery man appeared around the back they'd kick off, honking and hissing, and, if we'd left the gate open, charging their victim.

Duncan was the villain of the piece. He was one big beast of a gander, all neck, beak and testosterone. He once got Dad cornered in his own greenhouse. Luckily, Dad had the hosepipe connected up and was able to fight his way out behind a fierce jet of ice-cold water.

Once in a while, to our great delight, the whole gaggle would take flight, flapping in perfect V-formation down Crayke High Street, 'like a flight of Lancaster bombers', as Dad put it.

We never knew how Dad dispatched the Christmas goose every year. Or geese, I should say, because he generally sold one or two to neighbours. I'd seen him break many a young cockerel's neck – indeed, he'd taught me how to do it, and I got to be quite adept – but the goose was a different proposition. I never found out for sure, but I think an axe was involved. Whatever the case, we were generally presented with a row of headless corpses hanging from a beam in one of the outhouses and told to pluck them.

The first time we were given the job we thought it would be fun. We couldn't wait to get started, and of course had no time to listen to Mum's advice – something about hot water. No, we were in far too much of a hurry, hatching plans to make pillows or eiderdowns and sell them at the gate. We waded in as children will, and started yanking fistfuls of feathers and soft white down from the lifeless bodies.

It wasn't long before we were standing knee-deep in the stuff. The air in the shed was full of it, and we were spitting feathers off our lips, waving them away from our faces. They stuck to our clothes and hair, and worked their way into our ears and up our noses, making us sneeze. When Mum came to the door to see how we we're getting on, she couldn't help but laugh at us.

'What a sight! You look like four Eskimos lost in a blizzard. Come on,' she said, 'outside with you. Let's do what I told you in the first place.'

We cleaned ourselves up as well as we could and trudged back to the house, where she boiled up two big kettles of water. Then we carried them back to the shed and she poured the contents over the partly plucked birds.

'Now, isn't this a lot easier?' she said, pulling out handfuls of sodden feathers and dumping them on the table. Silence. Then, 'Well, what do we say?'

'Mum knows best,' we chorused.

'Yes,' she said, 'Mum knows best. And in future, just do what I tell you. There's usually a sound reason for it.'

Once you have animals living on the premises you have to be on the look-out for pests and predators. Whenever we suspected a rat was sniffing around the henhouse, Dad would lay poisoned bait in a clay land-drain and tuck it away under a board. We learned to keep the feed well covered up to keep the sparrows and starlings away, but of course the hens soon scattered it.

As it happened, the only one of our animals to suffer at the hands of a rat was our cat, Purdy. Purdy was a little demon when it came to catching mice, and was also an enthusiastic ratter. Perhaps she was too enthusiastic. One morning she appeared at the back door limping, and holding one of her front legs at a strange angle. It was badly swollen, and when we took her to the vet, she said that Purdy had been bitten by a rat. The wound had gone septic, and she needed to amputate the affected limb. After the operation Purdy changed. She still hunted mice, and she still purred like crazy, but she took to nudging you rhythmically as she purred, and dribbling. What the connection was we couldn't figure out, but it meant nobody wanted her snuggling up to them on the sofa.

But rats weren't our biggest worry. What we most feared was a fox getting into the hen run. We knew there was a fox living nearby, and suspected there might be family of them. We'd often hear the vixen barking in the night, and our suspicions were confirmed when we spotted a pair of them, and two tiny cubs, making their way to the rabbit warren that lay across the fields behind our property. We were extra-vigilant after that, making quite sure the hens were all locked up as soon as dusk fell. Quite how the fox got into the run was a mystery, but get in it did.

It's not a pleasant experience to come out on a morning to feed your hens and find their remains scattered all over the ground. For some reason a fox doesn't always take just what it can carry off. They seem to get caught up in the excitement of killing and will wipe out an entire flock. Some people think it's the noise of the hens squawking that panics them.

What I found that morning was truly sickening. There were feathers and body parts and whole dead fowl all over the place, and a solitary confused hen, trotting around and clucking in an agitated way. It looked genuinely distressed, and to our knowledge never laid another egg.

How the fox had got into the henhouse remained a mystery, but the door was swinging in the breeze, and when I ventured inside there was more carnage. Had we forgotten to lock up? Had somebody tampered with the latch? Or had the fox worked out how to undo it? We never came up with an answer.

Dad took it philosophically. Either that or he did an excellent job of appearing to.

'These things happen,' he said. 'It's Nature. You just have to accept it and carry on.'

So we re-stocked, fitted a stronger catch on the door, strengthened the fence all the way round and hoped that the local hunt would round up Mr Fox and his family. We all benefited hugely from keeping all the animals. It taught us a lot about responsibility. It taught us respect for Nature. And it taught us to cope with the ups and downs that the natural world throws at you.

Staying Warm

Dad was standing in the kitchen with a fourteen-pound sledgehammer in one hand and a cold chisel in the other. He had on a pair of brown corduroy trousers, a flat cap and a woolly jumper. We knew this meant business. It was what he called his battle dress, and when he put that on there was always some sort of excitement in the wind, usually involving loud noises.

'The first thing I'll need to do,' he said, 'is have this thing out.'

He was looking at the old range. He and Mum had tried to make it work when we first moved in, but all we got was a house full of smoke and some industrial-strength language.

Since then it had sat there, silent apart from the occasional sound of loose mortar falling down the chimney and pinging off its cast-iron casing.

'Might make a few pounds from the scrap man,' Dad added as he tapped it with his hammer.

Its day had come. Dad was going to demolish it. Another step in his campaign to make the house warmer. We all thought that was a good thing. When we moved in Beech House was a big, draughty place with rattling windows, ill-fitting doors, and no heat source other than the open fire in the living room. And keeping that fire in overnight was a constant battle. So his plan to install our first central heating system was good news. The bad news was, the house was going to get a lot colder first as he opened up holes in the chimney-breasts, the floorboards and the walls.

That was the year, too, when we all kept a potty under our bed, Mum having decided that it was simply too cold for us to be trailing outside to the toilet. So that was another morning job, creeping downstairs trying not to spill the contents.

But now it was all going to be different. It would, however, take a little time. Dad looked at Mum.

'Sorry, but there's going to be a lot of banging and crashing,' he said.

I had no idea why he was apologising. I couldn't imagine anything I'd rather do on a Saturday morning than help him smash the place up.

'I reckon most of this chimney-breast'll have to come out too. But I'll re-use the bricks, so they won't be wasted.'

I paused, halfway through my Shreddies. This was getting more interesting by the minute.

'I can help,' I said. 'I'm going to be a demolition man when I grow up.'

Before Dad could answer, Mum said, 'Do you really have to? It's going to make a horrible mess.' She sighed. 'I mean, why can't you get the builders in? Other people do.'

'I can help,' I said. 'It'd be good practice for me.'

Dad was ignoring me too.

'No,' he said, 'I've seen these contractors at work. They're not to be trusted. Soon as they've got their bit done they're off – and leave you to make good. They rip up floorboards and skirting-boards, bang holes through the wall. The place is never the same again. No, if we're going to have the place turned upside down I'd rather do it my own way. At least it'll be our mess, and we'll be able to fix it in due course.'

'I can help,' I repeated. 'I'm really good at knocking things down.'

'Oh, do be quiet,' Mum said. 'This isn't a game. You can help by eating up your breakfast and going out to play. I'm sure your father doesn't want you children under his feet all day.'

I slid off my chair, put my bowl in the old pot sink and stamped my way through to the living room. I could never understand grown-ups. Always going on about making yourself useful, and then when you offer to help they tell you you're in the way.

I slumped on the settee, between the girls. Oh well, at least it was Saturday morning. We could settle down and watch Multi-Coloured Swap Shop on the telly – or was it Banana Splits? Whatever it was I could guarantee Gillian would want something else. Still, it wasn't all bad news: a fight with my sister would liven things up.

The great central heating scheme would take a full calendar year and it would turn the place upside-down, just as Mum feared it would. But what fun it was – at least at the beginning.

Mum had decided that she didn't want to be around when the dust started flying. She took the bus into York and went shopping. Dad decided that he could use a willing pair of hands after all, and although my job wasn't exactly what I'd hoped for – it was he who climbed up the step-ladder and swung the fourteen-pound hammer, leaving me to collect the bricks off the floor and pile them in the wheelbarrow – I still felt I was in on the fun. I got to tie a handkerchief round my nose and mouth and pretend I was a bandit breaking into a bank vault, and that Dad was going to uncover a stack of gold bars and make us all rich.

The old range, he reckoned, hadn't been used in years, and as he dismantled the chimney, brick by brick, so he brought down an avalanche of soot, a tangle of old twigs – and a dead rook.

'Wow! Look at that!' I grabbed the bird, shook the dust off its threadbare wings and tried to open and close its beak. 'Can I have this, Dad? I can stuff it and take it into school and then it can go in a museum like that one we went to at Hutton le Hole. And maybe they'll put my name on it so that everyone'll know – '

'Ugh! Put it down. You'll catch ...' Christine had come into the kitchen and was pulling her I'm-about-to-bring-my-food-up face. 'It's disgusting, that is. You're bound to catch something. It's unclean.'

Phil had followed her in. 'Unclean, unclean,' he said. 'You'll catch the plague, won't he, Dad? The Black Death, most likely. Your face'll come out in big red blebs and you'll start choking and you'll have to go around ringing a bell to warn people. Unclean, unclean.'

'Yeah, and after that,' Christine said, 'you'll die a horrible death. This time next week we'll be digging you a special grave – about twenty feet deep so that nobody else catches it. They have special pits for plague victims. We learned about it on our trip to York.'

"Cos they're unclean … unclean …' When Phil got hold of an idea he hated to let go of it. As I dropped the dead bird to the floor Phil grinned and asked, 'Can you leave me your Thunderbirds collection in your will? To sell, like. I could do with a bit of extra cash. Go on, I'll write you a receipt right now.'

'Now then you two, enough of that.' Dad had come down off his stepladder. 'If you want to make yourselves useful I can find you a job.'

But they didn't. They were off. He turned to me and said, 'Don't worry, Michael, they're only trying to get you worked up.' He looked at the dead rook. 'But they have a point. You really shouldn't handle dead things without gloves on. Best stick it in the barrow, eh?'

It didn't take Dad long to do his part of the job. In fact, I could see why he'd chosen it: it was dead easy. The bricks came tumbling down in clusters as he swung his mighty hammer. I couldn't wait for him to slip out for a crafty smoke so that I could have a go. But he never did, not until he'd got it all down.

Barrowing the debris out into the yard was what took the time. After the first few runs my arms started aching and each load became gradually smaller and smaller. But we got there, and when Mum came home from town there was a huge expanse of bare brickwork where the chimney-breast used to be, and Dad was busy working out how to dismantle the range itself.

'My goodness. Look at you two.' Mum was shaking her head. 'And just look at my kitchen. It looks like a bomb's hit it.' She inspected her watch. 'And what are we going to do for our tea? I can't cook in here.'

Dad looked around the room, and ran a finger over the draining-board where the dust lay thick and black.

'This stuff gets everywhere, I'm afraid. I thought we'd all go for fish and chips.'

'I think we shall have to,' Mum said, 'but not until you two have hosed yourselves down.'

By this time I'd seen myself in the big hall mirror. I didn't want to get washed. I rather liked my new chimney-sweep look. My face was black, my hair was stiff with dust and had turned grey, and I had white rings around my eyes. I took out a filthy hanky and blew my nose. This was too good a chance to miss. I went into the sitting-room where the girls were watching gymnastics on Grandstand.

'Wanna see what came out of my nose?' I said. 'It's all black. Here.'

'Go away!' they shrieked.

Winding those girls up was a sure way to have a good laugh – and so easy. However, there was no chance of Mum letting me go to the chippy looking like this. I trudged across to the kitchen sink and turned on the tap. Nothing.

'Aha!' I said. 'Look, I can't wash. There's no water.'

'No water?' Mum looked at me, then at Dad. 'What've you done?'

'Ah,' he said. 'Safety precaution. Won't be a moment.' And with that he dived under the sink, picked up a huge spanner and restored the supply. 'Now go and get washed, as your mother told you,' he said.

This demolition job was just the beginning, a minor disruption amongst many more. Over the next few months – and right through another freezing winter – we learned to live with holes in the ceilings, holes in the walls and no-go areas where Dad had lifted the floor-boards to expose the black earth below us. Lengths of copper pipe lay along the hallway or were stacked in convenient corners. A collection of dusty radiators arrived in a van and were piled up in the kitchen by two mysterious men wearing donkey-jackets with leather shoulders. Dad said they were friends of his and he'd done a deal with them. All weekend, just about every weekend, sometimes right into the night, the house echoed to the sound of sawing and drilling, clanging and banging – not to mention the odd muffled curse as Dad struggled to remove hundred-year-old nails from thick, warped floorboards.

All through these upheavals, we did our best to stay warm, piling coal on the living room fire every night and sitting as close as we could without scorching ourselves. Yet no matter how near we were to the blaze, Purdy, Petra and Rosie always managed to squeeze their way in front of us to stare into the flames, half asleep, as we ran our hands over them to check that they hadn't actually caught fire.

Most nights Mum and Dad would damp the fire down with a bucketfull of coal dust. The idea was that all you had to do in the morning was give it a good poke and it would come back to life. That worked, most of the time, but when the wind was in a certain direction it would blaze up in the night and we'd come downstairs, shivering, to find a hearth full of pale grey ashes.

And so I learned how to light a fire from scratch, rolling up sheet after sheet of newspaper and making little doughnut-shaped rings, adding whatever sticks I could find around the place, and carefully piling small pieces of coal on top. I learned, too, to get a good draught by holding a big sheet of newspaper across the fireplace – and to let go, quickly, when it went up in flames.

Sometimes I managed the boy-scout trick, lighting the fire with a single match. Sometimes I failed. What I wanted was to be allowed to use the paraffin can that was stored in the outhouse, but I knew that was against the rules. Rules, however, are made to be broken.

It was a Sunday morning, and a very cold one. It wasn't quite light when I woke up. Everybody else was fast asleep, or pretending to be. I pulled back the curtain a few inches and saw frost patterns all over the window. I leaned forward, opened my mouth and breathed out, melting a small circle to see through. Outside the trees were decorated a ghostly white. There was a long icicle hanging from the overflow pipe that jutted out from the wall of the privy. I shivered, put on a sweater and my slippers, picked up my pot from under the bed, and went downstairs to stir the fire into life.

Whoever had banked it up the night before had clearly overdone it. They'd suffocated it. Just to make sure, I took the poker and thrust it into the mound of lifeless coal-dust. Nothing. Just a minor landslide that formed a conical pile on the cold hearth. With my teeth chattering, I weighed up the chances of getting the fire going again without rebuilding it, completely. No. It wouldn't work.

I went to the foot of the stairs and listened. There was a gentle, rhythmic snoring coming from Mum and Dad's room. Otherwise all was silent. Purdy slid past my bare leg as I turned around, went to the back door, unlocked it and made my way to the outhouse. I opened the door as quietly as I could, picked up the can of paraffin, and hurried back indoors, grinning as I imagined how grateful they'd all be for this, waking up to a blazing fire and a nice warm house. I sloshed paraffin into the fireplace and watched it disappear into the mound of black dust. Maybe a little more then. Splosh. Which also vanished. One more for luck. Splosh. I put the can to one side and reached up to the mantelpiece for the matches.

I must have mentioned it earlier, how I like a good fire. The bigger the flames, the better. This one was a five-star job. I struck the red-headed match on the brick surround, just the way a cowboy would, leaving a long red streak. It flared into life. I leaned forward and applied it to the moribund fire. There was a deep, soft whoomph! and up she went, a column of yellow flames that reached out and singed my eyebrows before roaring up the chimney.

I stayed where I was for a minute or two, glorying in the success of my efforts. Then I darted into the hallway. Maybe I ought to wake Phil and show him what I'd managed to do. But then I thought, no, all the better if he comes down late and sees me with a plate full of hot buttered toast, stuffing myself.

I squatted down at the hearth once more, reaching out my hands, relishing the warmth that enveloped me. Then I went out to the kitchen pantry, cut myself a fat slice of bread and dug out the toasting-fork. Armed with that, and the butter, I waited for the flames to settle down.

I was dimly conscious of a strange, muffled roaring sound coming from the chimney, but assumed it was nothing more than the draught – always a sign of a good fire, Dad said.

It was only when a big lump of something soft fell onto the fire and landed in the grate, smothering my bread, that the first wave of doubt washed through me. I looked at the little red dots that danced over the scattered soot. Oh dear, I thought. Oh dear.

I dashed into the kitchen and headed for the back door, but I didn't need to go outside. Through the window I could see a turbid yellow-and-grey fog tumbling down from above and swamping the yard.

I raced into the hallway and took the stairs three at a time.

'Mum! Dad!' I shouted. 'The chimney's on fire! Quick! The whole house is going to – '

Fortunately for me, Dad was at his imperturbable best. He appeared at his bedroom door just as Phil, Gillian and Christine spilled out onto the landing. 'Let's have a look, shall we?' And he walked calmly down the stairs, fastening his thick dressing gown around him. The others followed, Mum too. Phil dashed ahead, poked his head into the living room, then turned back and looked at me.

'You've done it now,' he said. 'You've really done it, mate.'

The others followed him into the room. They looked frightened. Sleepy but frightened.

Dad took a look at the fire, and the small mound of soot that had now spilled all over the hearth. He crouched down and tried to look up the chimney, but the heat drove him back.

'Well,' he said, 'it looks as though you could be right, Michael. About the chimney, I mean. But it's built of good sturdy bricks. The house should be all right.'

Then he stared at it for a moment more, let out a thoughtful 'ah', and turned on his heel, making for the back door.

I followed him outside into the yard, shivering with fear as much as the cold, and coughing as the thick, tarry cloud filled the air around us. The others clustered in the doorway, wafting the smoke away from their faces. Petra shot out from the kitchen and darted down the yard, her tail between her legs. Rosie followed. Dad was walking slowly backwards, trying to get a good view of the chimney.

'Well, your diagnosis is correct,' he said. 'It's well ablaze. Come on, inside with you or you'll freeze to death. We need to get on the phone.'

What followed was about as exciting as a Sunday could get in those days, when everything was shut all day and the highlight – after the roast dinner and a steamed pudding – was some ancient black-and-white film or The Big Match. I remember standing and watching as Dad dialled the magical number, 9 … 9 … 9, waiting to hear what he said. I remembered how Phil had dared me to do it one time in the public call-box just across the way, and called me chicken when I refused. Dad was through to the fire brigade and explaining, very calmly, that we had a chimney fire – and no, there was nobody in danger, and he thought that it might burn itself out, but there were the neighbours to think of. I couldn't believe he was being so calm. In books, when a chimney caught fire, everything went up in smoke and the chapter always ended with a little drawing of a pile of charred timbers and a curlicue of smoke. Now we stood there, watching in rapt silence as Dad replaced the receiver.

Nobody spoke – not aloud, that is; but Phil whispered in my ear, 'You're gonna be in for it, you are. Trying to burn the house down. I wouldn't want to be in your shoes.'

I didn't need Phil to tell me that trouble was brewing. It always seemed to when I tried to help, but right now I was far more concerned with the imminent arrival of a big, red, shiny fire-engine. I'd seen one at Malton Show the previous summer and added 'fireman' to the growing list of things I wanted to be when I left school. The idea of one coming to our house, bells ringing, was making me shake all the more – with anticipation rather than cold this time.

'When d'you think it'll get here?' I asked. 'Will they be sliding down that pole now, d'you think? Will they put a ladder up?' No answer. 'And where will they get the water from? Will it mean they put the fire out too?'

I was concerned about the fire. It seemed to me that even if I was punished for setting the chimney ablaze I ought to get some credit for getting such a good fire going.

'Oh, do be quiet, Michael.' Mum grabbed hold of my shoulders and steered me towards the foot of the stairs. 'Go and get dressed, and the rest of you. I don't want an army of firemen trooping in here and thinking I let you lie in bed all morning.'

Dad looked at his watch.

'To be fair, dear,' he said, 'it is Sunday and it is only twenty past seven.'

But Mum was in a determined frame of mind.

'Never mind that, you children do as I say. Now.'

There were no bells, which was a disappointment, and the first we knew that the fire brigade had arrived was when they knocked on the front door and asked us if we had any carpets to take up, because they were going to put water down the chimney. Luckily, Dad had been working on a pipe-run in the living room, so it was bare boards in there. I watched, fascinated, as the men in uniform unwound the great fat hose, extended the ladder, and sent one of their number up to the chimney with the hose trailing behind him. When he gave the order there was a lot of hissing, a huge cloud of steam blew into the front room, and there was a fireman commandeering the wheelbarrow and loading it up with a sodden mound of hot soot.

The fire tender wasn't with us for more than half an hour or so, and I wasn't able to get into the cab as I had at Malton Show, but as our neighbours gathered around it I stood there telling the tale of how it all came about. I was re-telling it for the third time, and starting to paint myself as the hero of the hour, when Mum came out, clipped me round the ear and told me to get back inside and start cleaning up the mess I'd caused.

Dad eventually got the heating system rigged up in time for the following winter, and replaced the open fire with a log-burner for high days and holidays.

As we revelled in the novelty of having warm, dry towels, constant hot water and an actual shower over the bath, there was a bit of excitement when the lads who'd delivered the cheap radiators featured in a newspaper story about thefts from a warehouse down at a trading estate on the outskirts of York, but Dad assured Mum that ours were from a reputable source. Those fellows, he said, were just the delivery team. I don't think she believed him, but she settled for that version of events and it was never mentioned again.

So now we were fully up to date, and friends called in to marvel at the hot radiators – and the fact that we could play in our rooms in midwinter and take our coats off.

My punishment for setting the chimney on fire? Well, that was an odd one. I was actually barred from one of the chores that everyone else moaned about: early-morning fire duties.

The Mysterious Hut

I don't know why it took us so long to discover the place. We'd been going to Staintondale for our holidays for as long as we could remember, and it seemed as though we'd always been left free to explore the surrounding woods and fields, and the many byways that led off the path that wound down to Hayburn Wyke. But somehow we'd never come across the hut before.

It wasn't new – or certainly didn't look as though it was. At first sight it had a decidedly abandoned appearance. Dilapidated, you might say. It may be that it had been hidden by the tangle of roses and elder trees that surrounded its particular corner of the field, and that the farmer had now grubbed out a bit of hedge, exposing it to view. Or it may have been the winter storm that swept across the north and took out so many old trees.

But whatever the case, the fact remained that for all the times we'd cut across the field on our way to the clifftop where the brambles would stop a tank, according to Billy, and the berries were the size of your granny's thimble, we'd never spotted it.

'Cor, look at that!'

Phil almost bumped into me as I stopped, dropped my basket in the grass and stared. All that was visible amongst the thicket of trees and bushes was a squat brick chimney poking through a low-pitched roof that appeared to be covered in felt rather than slates. But as we approached the overgrown thorn hedge we saw a low, squat building, built of wood and painted green – the dark green of a holly tree.

'Hmm. Never seen that before.'

Phil put his basket down next to mine and set off across the field, leaping from one tussock to the next.

'Come on,' he shouted over his shoulder, 'let's have a look.'

As I approached it I saw that there was a faint path trodden in the grass. It was no wider than a rabbit run at first, but it broadened out slightly, as we drew near to the place, and led to an old iron gate, quite a small one, set between a pair of metal posts. One was topped with ivy. The other was bare, and rusty. A solitary crow was perched on it. As we hesitated, it looked at us, then flew from its perch and settled on the dead branch of a large oak-tree that loomed over the little enclosure.

Phil walked slowly towards the gate. I followed, several paces behind him.

'You – you don't think it's haunted, do you?' I said.

'Nah,' he said. But there was a distinct hesitation before he added, 'Don't be daft.'

Phil had reached the gate. Beyond him I could already see the door of the hut. It too was made of boards, but vertical ones, bare and sun-bleached. To either side of it was a small rectangular window, shaded by matching curtains.

'D'you think anyone lives here?' I whispered.

Phil didn't answer. He was approaching the door, his hand out ready to grasp the hexagonal metal handle. I waited at the gate, my heart thumping. The crow squawked and flew off into the woods.

'Let's go,' I said. 'I don't like this. There might be – you know, ghosts and things.'

Phil gave a nervous little laugh.

''S all right,' he said. 'Ghosts don't come out until it gets dark. Midnight.' Then he added, 'It's the zombies you want to worry about.'

But his jaunty air wasn't very convincing. As much as trying to scare me he was also attempting to fortify himself. I looked around the field. Were we being watched? I had an awful feeling that we were. Turning back to look at the hut I found myself rooted to the spot, my mouth agape. I wanted to shout out a warning, but I seemed unable to speak. The curtain at the right-hand window had moved to one side and a face – a wrinkled face surrounded by a shock of white hair – peered through the murky glass. Then a hand appeared and four bony fingers started to wipe the dirt away.

We reacted as one, turning and running full pelt – out through the gateway, across the field and heading for home. We didn't stop till we could see the farmhouse, and there was Petra running out to meet us. It occurred to me that we should've had her with us. Dogs can sense ghosts. At least, that's what I'd heard. Somewhere.

Left to our own devices, we probably wouldn't have gone back that way for the rest of the holiday. But we'd no sooner got home than we realised we'd left the baskets behind. And hadn't Doris sent us out specifically to get some blackberries for a pie she was baking that afternoon? And hadn't she reminded us that the best berries we ever got were from the hedges around that field?

'What we going to do?' I said.

Phil shrugged. 'Looks like we'd better go back,' he said. Then he laughed and added, 'Better bring your bow and arrow, eh?'

I didn't take the bow, but I did make sure I'd a got a few decent-sized stones in my trouser pockets. And I carried a stout stick. So did Phil. And this time we had Petra with us. Her presence gave us both a bit of extra courage. Even so, we made our way back in silence.

As we climbed over the wooden stile we could see the hut quite plainly, and wondered again how we'd managed to miss it in the past. We dropped into the field and stood there for a moment. I looked around, hoping to see the baskets, but the grass was too long. Petra had already scampered away to the far side, where the rabbits were.

I followed Phil into the field, one eye scanning the ground, the other watching out for any movement from the direction of the haunted hut, as I now thought if it. We edged cautiously forward, following the line of flattened grass we'd made earlier. So where were the baskets? We drew closer to the hedge that bordered the field. Had we gone past them?

'Maybe somebody's picked them up,' I said.

I desperately wanted Phil to agree, so that we could go home. We could make up some excuse easily enough.

'How about we tell Auntie Doris that some big boys came and stole them?' I suggested.

Phil didn't like that. ''S going to make us look a right couple of fairies, isn't it?' he said. 'Come on, they'll be here somewhere.'

'I say, are you looking for these?'

The voice sounded dead posh. But when I turned around the figure I saw looked like a tramp – or what I thought a tramp ought to look like. He had a grubby pair of leather shoes, one of which had a hole in the toe, a pair of loose-fitting khaki trousers with grass-stained knees, a baggy sweater with splashes of red and yellow paint down the front. In his hands he held our baskets. His fingers were long and thin. I looked up to see his face, framed by a straw hat and … the same untidy mop of thin white hair I'd seen at the window barely an hour previously.

'It's him!' I shouted, and started running.

I'd got halfway to the stile when I paused to look back. Phil was standing where I'd left him. Petra was beside him, rolling in the grass at the stranger's feet. If there was one thing we could always rely on, it was Petra's sense of who we could trust and who we couldn't. If that old man had represented any danger to us she would have circled him, hackles raised, growling, and even gone for his ankles. But there she was, picking herself to take some kind of treat from his hand.

'It's all right,' Phil called, waving his arm. 'Come back.'

I stayed where I was for a moment, trying to get my breath back. Then I made my way slowly towards him. The old fellow was talking to Phil. He reached down and ruffled the hair on Petra's throat.

Then he turned to me, smiled, and said, 'Allow me to introduce myself. Augustus Proudfoot, artist.' With that he held out his hand and before I knew it I'd grasped and shaken it. 'Artist and occasional hermit,' he added. 'But you may call me Gus. I live in the hut there. During my holidays, you understand.'

I looked at Phil, pulling a face that was supposed to reflect my confusion. Maybe the guy was still a maniac, but a very clever one. Phil seemed equally uncertain.

'Yeah,' he said, 'me and my brother here were just – '

'Aha!' The man handed Phil the baskets. 'Brambling, no doubt. Now, if you care to follow me towards the rear of my rude shelter you'll find some of the fattest, sweetest berries you've ever tasted.'

I looked at Phil. I was quite prepared to make a dash for it. Maybe this was one of those molesters we'd been warned about, a weirdo. But if so, why was Petra so unconcerned?

'Ah,' he said, looking us up and down. 'I see. I dare say you think me a strange sort of chap.' He gave a gentle chuckle. 'Well, I'm a painter you see. We're all a bit odd. Take no notice of the garb. Wouldn't do to wear your best clothes to work in, would it now?'

We didn't answer. We just stared. Petra, meanwhile, had wandered towards the hut, her nose to the ground.

'Look, if you come to the garden gate you'll see my easel and oils. Then you can go round the back on your own and pick away to your hearts' content. How's that?' He glanced at us, then tilted his head back and looked at the sky. 'Meanwhile, I shall continue the eternal quest to capture on canvas the subtly shifting contours of the fair-weather cumulus.'

Phil and I looked at each other. He'd got us both in a flat spin.

'Cumulus,' he repeated, and pointed skyward. 'It's those puffy white clouds you see there. From the Latin, meaning pile. See how they're sort of piled up, do you?'

Mister Augustus Proudfoot – it was some time before we learned to call him Gus – did indeed have an easel in his overgrown garden, and on it was indeed a painting of a cloud, just like the one that was passing over the hut as we stood there. And when we went around the back we did indeed find a crop of brambles that were huge, sweet and abundant.

We filled our baskets, shouted goodbye and hurried home. Doris was at the kitchen window as we walked into the yard. She came to the door to meet us.

'I was beginning to wonder where you two had got to,' she said. 'I've been baking all afternoon. The oven's ready, and the pastry.' She looked into the baskets. 'Ooh, my goodness aren't they beautiful? All we need now is a few apples. If I add a few early wind-falls they'll most likely make two pies. Well done, the pair of you.'

'Sorry we took so long,' Phil said, 'but there was this – '

'Yeah, there was this old bloke,' I said, 'and he was right weird, all covered in paint and his fingers were like – like talons,' I said. It was a new word I'd got from a book about birds of prey. 'And he lives in this old shack in the woods.'

Doris had been frowning at me as I spoke, her face lined with concentration. Then it broke into a smile.

'Oh, so you met our Mister Proudfoot, did you? Such an interesting man! A little eccentric, I suppose, but a lovely fellow all the same.'

'You know him?' Phil asked.

'Oh, we all know Mister Proudfoot. He's been amongst us for a long time now. You know, we really feel it's a bit of an honour having him here. He's a very well known artist. He's exhibited in London. The Royal Academy, they say.'

She took the baskets from us and wheeled away into the kitchen. We followed her inside, drawn partly by curiosity, partly by the smell of whatever she was baking.

'I could tell you lots about our Augustus.' She pointed to the painting on the wall, a view of the country around Staintondale with sheep dotting the grass. 'He painted this, and gave it to us. Years ago now.'

She sat us down at the table, poured us each a glass of milk, and went to open the oven.

'Ah, perfect,' she said, and pulled out a tray of flapjacks. 'I'll just pop them on the rack.'

While they cooled she told us Mister Proudfoot's story.

'He grew up around here, you see, and everybody knew he was gifted. He must have been about eighteen when he went off to the big city to make his fortune.'

'Fortune?' I repeated. 'D'you mean he's rich?'

'Doesn't look it,' Phil said.

Doris smiled.

'No, he looks more like a tramp – when he's working. You see, he taught at an art school for years and then when he retired he bought that little place you've seen and uses it in the summer. There's no electricity, nor running water. Wouldn't suit me, but ... Each to their own, as they say.' She went to the counter and held the back of her hand over the flapjacks. 'Ah, that's cool enough for two growing lads,' she said. As she laid them on a plate and brought them to the table she said, 'But I'm surprised you've not met him before – although to tell the truth we hardly ever catch sight of him either. Sometimes on a morning, if we go out for mushrooms, we'll see him with his easel. He's always up early. In fact, many a night he sleeps out under the stars.'

'Wow,' I said, 'that must be fun.'

Doris shivered. 'When you're young, maybe. When you get to my age you prefer a nice feather eiderdown and a sprung mattress.'

'But he's old – same as you, I mean.'

As I spoke Phil kicked me under the table.

Doris laughed. 'Out of the mouths of babes and sucklings,' she said. 'Yes, he is indeed as old as me. Older, in fact, if you can imagine such a thing. We were at school with him, but he was a few years above us. So, quite ancient, I suppose. Thing is, he's an artist. They're not like the rest of us. As you'll find out, if you get talking to him.'

Now that we knew he wasn't a weirdo, or a murderer on the run – or a ghost – we did get to talk to Mister Proudfoot. In fact, we called on him again the very next day – supposedly to pick more berries, but really we were drawn back there because we wanted to know more about this unusual man. He knew by now where we came from, word having reached him on the bush telegraph, as it were, and he confirmed that he'd known Doris and the rest of them since he was a lad.

He showed us inside his little cabin. It was no more than a single large room. At one end was a table, all covered with paper and paints, brushes in pots, all except one corner. There sat a plate, a mug and a sharp knife. Looking around I saw no sign of a sink, a cooker or a bed, just more artists' materials: books, canvases, drawings, paintings – some finished, some half-done and apparently abandoned – and a clutter of interesting instruments, including a telescope, a paraffin lamp and an old-fashioned bellows-type camera on a black metal tripod.

'Yes,' he said, as he shifted a pile of canvases from a rickety stool and invited me to sit down, leaving Phil to lean against the door-jamb, 'it's what you might call a shade primitive. The privy's at the back if you need it. The little shed. There's a pump out there too, for my water. As for cooking, I prefer to do that on a camp fire.'

He walked across to the far end of the room and tapped on what looked like a shutter of some sort.

'And this,' he said, ' folds down to make me a bed – when I'm not sleeping *sous la belle étoile*, as the French like to say.'

'*Sous* what?' I said.

'In the – ah, in the open,' Gus replied. 'You should try it sometime, the pair of you. See if the good ladies can't lend you an old blanket or two. We could light a fire, fry some sausages and watch the moon rise. Or set.' He went and rummaged through some papers on the table. 'I have a chart here somewhere with all the phases on it – and the tides.

Anyway, I expect you'll need what we used to call a leave pass, won't you? From the dear old ladies. Or your parents.'

We asked Mum and Dad that same evening. Mum looked doubtful, but Doris and the others confirmed that Gus was a reliable and trustworthy fellow, and a couple of days later, around teatime, we set out with our supplies. We had a back-pack each, with sausages, bread, a newly baked cake and some bottles of pop. The sky was clear and, according to Dad, a full moon would rise just after sunset, which was around eight-thirty. We arrived at the hut just as Gus was cutting the grass, not with a lawnmower but with an old, long-handled scythe.

'Good exercise, this,' he said, pausing to lean on his tool and wipe the sweat from his forehead. 'Builds up a fellow's appetite.' He looked at us and said, 'Hungry?'

'Yes,' we chorused.

'Brought any food?'

'Yes.'

'Well, we'd better get a fire going, hadn't we? No mod cons in the cabin, I'm afraid.' He picked up an armful of dead wood from a pile he had lying in the grass. 'You boys know all about lighting fires, I suppose?'

Phil laughed and pointed at me. 'He does. He set the chimney on fire.'

'Oh dear. Just trying to help, I dare say.' He looked at me and winked. 'Eh?'

Then he set about laying the fire, building a latticework of straight twigs that he piled up several inches high before dropping some dry material into the centre.

'Now,' he said, 'there you have the Proudfoot patent method. One match and she should be away.'

He reached into his trouser pocket, pulled out a red-top match and held it out.

'So who's to do it? Perhaps you, Philip. Being the elder.' Then he nudged me. 'Your turn next time, young fellow.'

Phil struck the match and held it to the pile. It caught immediately, and within minutes we had a good blaze going, with Gus piling heavier bits of wood around it to make a cone-shaped fire.

'Now,' he said, 'the trick is to be patient. We want to burn up a good lot of wood, then let it die down. Some people get too impatient and end up with their food all smoky. This way we'll have a bed of hot coals, with no fumes. Just perfect for cooking – what is it you've brought?'

'Bangers,' I said.

'Ah, perfect. And I have the beans.' He rubbed his hands together. 'We'll have a rare old feast.'

We sat for a long time, stacking more timber on the fire, letting it burn, adding some more. Then, finally, Gus said we had enough. We'd let it die down. By the time he pronounced the fire ready, there was just this low mound of glowing coals. He pulled out three long sticks, each one sharpened at the end.

'My home-made toasting-forks,' he said, and handed us one apiece. 'Now, spear yourself a sausage each – two if you think you can manage it – and start cooking. I'd better open the beans, hadn't I?'

He poured them into a saucepan and set it beside the fire. Within a minute or two one side of it was bubbling. He picked up a green stick, peeled the bark off, and stirred. Meanwhile we tried to find the best position for our sausages, exclaiming with delight when the fat spurted out of them and ignited.

'Like a flame-thrower,' Phil said. 'Could be a new secret weapon.'

By now the sun had disappeared behind the surrounding bushes and Gus was looking at his watch.

'Another half hour or so and we should see the moon coming up,' he said.

He glanced at the sky, which had turned a delicate pale blue. There were just a couple of golden wisps of cloud. A flight of birds, in V formation, flew across our field of vision, heading inland.

'Aah,' Gus sighed. 'Couldn't have asked for a better night, could we?'

We mumbled agreement, our mouths crammed full of sausages. They tasted better than any I'd ever had. Juices dribbled down our chins and wrists as we tried to eat one and cook the next at the same time. As we finished them off and scraped the last of the beans from the pot, Gus got to his feet and said, 'Time to see where that moon's got to.'

We went out into the field. I think that was the first time I'd ever stood and watched the moon rise. It came up fat and red and huge. It was almost frightening, certainly awe-inspiring. Gus explained that it wasn't enlarged at all, just that it always appeared so on the horizon. I wasn't convinced. It seemed to me that it was a giant moon, its size fitted to the excitement of this special night.

We watched it for quite some time, our red faces cooled by a gentle on-shore breeze which carried the smell of seaweed and the rhythmic swish of the waves landing on the rocks below the cliff. Bats were darting around us in pursuit of their insect prey. A fox yipped in the distance. As the moon rose in the sky so it lost its pink colour and grew brighter, its light almost painful to the eye.

'The only drawback to a moon like that,' Gus said, 'is that you won't be able to see the stars so well. It outshines most of them. Otherwise you'd see the Milky Way. Still, we can't have everything, can we?' We agreed that you couldn't. 'Mind you,' he added, 'we can have crumpets. Would you like that?'

We hurried back into the garden and sat down by the fire. Gus handed out the crumpets and we toasted them as we'd cooked the sausages, our faces illuminated by the red glow. Once we'd dealt with those Gus fetched a garden rake and gathered up all the bits of half burned wood to re-kindle the fire.

'That'll give us a bit more light,' he said. 'Best capitalise on it and get our beds organised, don't you think?' He waved away a small cloud of midges that had gathered around us. 'Tell you what,' he said, 'you boys gather a few handfuls of long grass from over there.'

'What for?' I asked.

'You'll see.'

When we brought him what he'd asked for he set it down beside the fire and threw a few tufts onto the hot coals. Immediately a column of thick white smoke rose into the night air and spread across the little garden, hanging over it in thick skeins.

'Those midges can't stand smoke,' Gus said. 'This'll scatter them while we get ready for bed, eh?'

We unrolled our blankets, spreading them on the grass. Gus had an old eiderdown, but before he laid it out he went and got a garden spade. With that in his hand he surveyed an area of grass near the fire, lay down on his side, wriggled around, turned over and wriggled some more, then got up. He peered at the little patch he'd flattened. Then he struck it with the spade, squatted down and dug a shallow depression no thicker than the turf he lifted out.

'What's that you're doing?' Phil asked.

'Ah. It's an old trick I learned with the Chindits,' he said. 'When we were chasing the Japanese across Burma. We marched two thousand miles in hobnailed sandals carrying our full kit, and every night we had to sleep in the jungle. Just imagine. Night after night when you're worn out from marching you have to make camp, mount a guard and hope you don't get bitten to death by the insects.' He shuddered. 'My goodness, they had some fearsome bugs out there. But hey ho. Worse things happen at sea, as they say.' He pointed to the little hollow. 'Anyway, one thing I learned was that the worst part of camping, what bothered me most – apart from the mosquitoes, that is – was my hipbone. Used to ache like billy-ho. It was an Irishman, a soldier some years my senior, who told me the answer. First thing when you're sleeping out, he said: make a hollow for your hip. You'll be a lot more comfortable. Probably wouldn't trouble supple young fellows like you, but …' He tailed off, unrolled his cover, and settled down. 'If I start snoring,' he said, 'you just wake me up, won't you?' He settled down, then said, 'That same Irishman had us in stitches one night. We had a plague of fireflies. Lovely things and perfectly harmless, but after weeks of beating off the mosquitoes, old Paddy sits up and shouts, 'Bejasus! Now dey're coming at us wid searchlights!'

Phil and I snuggled down under our blankets, using our empty back-packs as pillows. The grass was soft and springy. The fire was slowly dying, but each breath of wind stirred the ashes and sent a ripple of red through them, and an odd spark drifted up into the sky. Above us was the bright round moon and a thin scattering of stars.

I remembered something Dad had told me, about how ancient people got to know them all and had names for every constellation. I could make out the Plough, at least, but that was it. Jack had taught me that one night when we were in the farmyard – and told me how you could locate the North Star from it. But I'd forgotten that already. I lay there in silence, hoping to see a meteorite.

I was loving this new experience, the cool night breeze caressing my face, my body snug and warm under the blanket. I lay awake for what seemed like hours.

'Phil?'

'Yeah?'

'Wass the time?'

I heard him wriggle around, untangling his blanket and freeing his arm. 'Er, half-past ten.'

'Oh.'

'What's up?'

'I thought it was midnight.'

'Nah. Nowhere near it. You wanna be asleep by then.'

'Why?'

Phil laughed. 'Because that's when the vampires come out.'

Trust my big brother to try and unsettle me. But as it happened I did fall asleep pretty quickly after that. I was reassured by Gus' steady breathing, and the fire, which seemed to be dozing rather than expiring. Surely ghosts and the like were scared of firelight?

I awoke before the sun had cleared the hedge top. Phil was still fast asleep but Gus had thrown some dry twigs on the fire and was poking it back to life.

'Ready for a spot of breakfast?' he asked.

He'd rigged up a sort of metal tripod and suspended from it a blackened kettle.

'There. We should be able to brew up some tea before too long.'

While we waited for the water to boil Gus started packing up an easel and some brushes.

'It looks a perfect day for a seascape,' he said. 'Nice breeze to put a bit of life into it, a few white-caps. I've a little spot on the cliff-top, just below the path,' he said. 'Spend hours and hours down there and, do you know, I've never been disturbed.'

After Phil woke up we drank our tea, polished off the last of the crumpets, and rolled up our beds.

'Well,' Gus said, 'it's been a pleasure having you boys to share my little hideaway. I don't often have company here. You must call by again some time.'

And with that he was off, through the gate and across the field with his painter's equipment bouncing on his stooped back.

We watched him go, then made our way home. Neither of us spoke. We knew we'd experienced something special, and each of us absorbed it in our own way.

Friday Tea

It was Friday. It was teatime. In fact, it was past teatime. Dad had come home from work and gone straight down the garden to sow his broad beans. Mum was in town shopping. We were all on the sofa watching children's television. As soon as the news came on we turned it off and headed into the kitchen, where we shared out the last few slices of bread, and the scrapings from a jar of home-made raspberry jam.

Just then Mum staggered in through the back door carrying three bags of shopping in each hand.

'What's for tea?' I mumbled the words through a mouthful of bread.

'Tea?' she said, a look of alarm on her face. 'Oh dear. I never gave it a thought. How about beans on toast?'

'Beans on toast?' Christine said. 'But we're starving.'

'Me too,' Mum said, and dumped the week's groceries on the kitchen table. 'But at least you lot had your school dinners. I've been on the go all day. Never had time for a bite.'

'It was rotten old mince for school dinner,' I said. 'I hate mince.'

Mum looked at her watch. 'And I've a Guides meeting tonight. Oh dear. Well, there's simply no time to cook. We'll just have to manage, that's all.' She looked at the four of us. 'Unless anyone wants to volunteer,' she said. 'Anyone?'

Phil and I backed away from her. The girls stood their ground. They knew they were safe: they had to help Mum at Girl Guides. It was us she was after.

'Dad said never volunteer for anything,' Phil said.

Mum laughed. 'Oh, did he? I can't think where he got that from.

Most likely your Grandpa. Typical old soldier.'

'Anyway,' Phil said, 'what we volunteering for?'

'Ah, that's for me to know and you to find out,' Mum said. 'But here's a hint.' She took her purse from her handbag and pulled out a crisp green £1 note. She reached forward, holding it under our very noses. 'Come on, you can keep the change. How about that for a deal?'

Before Phil could make a move, I grabbed it. Then I asked, 'What is it? What's the job?'

'Get your bike,' she said. 'I want you to go and fetch … fish and chips. One of each six times.'

'Oh great!' Phil shouted. 'Fish and chips! Fantastic!'

'And scraps!' Christine said. Then she gave me a shove. 'Go on, get a move on. Before we all die of hunger.'

'What, you want me to ride my Chopper all the way to Easingwold? That's miles.'

'Nah,' Phil said. 'Use my old one – and clip the basket on the front.'

'But Easingwold?'

Phil gave me a shove. 'Easy-peasy,' he said. It's two and a half miles. You can be there and back in … I dunno, just get your skates on,' he added as I made for the door. 'We don't want 'em going cold.'

I ran outside and took the bike from the garage. I checked the basket was securely in place and set off. As I pedalled furiously down the hill I tried to do the sums in my head. How much was one of each? And if I got six portions, how much change would there be?

Easingwold Church bell was sounding the half hour as I sped up to the little parade of shops and hurled my bike to the ground.

'One of each six times!' I blurted out as I ran inside.

A row of stern, hungry faces turned to stare at me. Men in overalls, women with their hair in curlers, and a couple of mothers with young children were lined up from the counter all the way to the door.

'You wait your turn, lad,' the lady at the till said. 'We'll serve the workers first if you don't mind.'

194

I tagged on to the end of the queue and caught my breath.

'Sorry,' I mumbled.

Slowly the queue edged forward. We were all watching every move as slippery white portions of fish were dipped in batter and dropped into the hot fat. There was a sharp intake of breath as the shout went up from behind the fryer, 'Out of cod!'

I watched as a stout woman bent over and scooped handfuls of fresh-cut chips into a wire basket and handed it to the head fryer. He lowered it into the fat, then pulled out a basket of partially cooked ones, squeezed a sample between his thumb and forefinger. 'Nearly there,' he said.

At the head of the counter another woman was handing a stack of wrapped suppers about three feet high to a customer. The man in front of me in the queue pulled a face and said, 'I hope she's left some for t'rest of us.'

'Be a few minutes for the cod,' the big man behind the counter said. 'Anyone want fishcakes?' There was a shaking of heads.

The longer I waited the more my stomach rumbled. The smell of frying, the sight of all those golden chips piled up behind the transparent covers, the tang of vinegar being splashed over yet another portion. It was torment.

Another satisfied customer peeled away. He had his supper open on the paper in his hand. As he edged past me he held it out to me. 'Go on, son, grab yourself a chip.'

I pulled out a long, fat one and shoved it in my mouth. 'Thanks,' I said, breathing sharply in to cool my tongue.

I was near the head of the queue now. Just three in front of me. I leaned on the hot shiny steel and gazed at the crispy battered fish, my mouth watering. One by one they were taken out, then replaced with fresh ones, plucked from the seething beef dripping.

'Yes, lad. What can we do for you?'

It was my turn at last.

'One of each six times with scraps,' I said.

The man at the counter grinned and said, 'Why, you must be a hungry, lad.' He didn't seem to expect an answer.

One or two people chuckled as he took his metal scoop and shovelled out a pile of chips. I said nothing. I was all eyes on what he was doing. He placed the fish on top of the chips. I was hoping to see which fish was the biggest, and try to make sure I collared it, but they all looked the same. I watched fascinated as he repeated his choreographed routine, while his assistant sprinkled the vinegar, then the salt.

'And scraps, you said?'

'Yes please.'

Someone in the queue laughed and said, 'Why, he's nowt but a scrap himself.'

I moved to the till. It was time to hand over my pound note. How much change would there be?

'That'll be six times twenty,' said the lady. 'That's one-twenty to you, lad.'

'But me Mum only gave me a pound.'

I'd had it in my hand since I ran into the shop. It was warm and damp from sweat. I held it out to him, aware that all eyes in the shop were on me.

'Aye, well, they've gone up since she was last in. Inflation.' She took the note. 'Where d'you live, lad?'

'Crayke,' I said.

'And they've sent you all this way on your bike?'

'Yes.'

'Been a bad lad have you? What was it, breaking the greenhouse window?'

Everyone laughed. 'No,' I said. 'I volunteered. They said I could keep the change.'

More laughter. 'Well, they sold you a right dummy, lad.' She picked up the white packages. 'What do they call you?'

'Michael ... Michael Pannett.'

'Right then, Michael Pannett, what you'll have to do – are you listening? – is take this lot home and bring me the money tomorrow. We open at midday. Can you do that?' She looked around at the customers. 'Plenty of witnesses, mind.'

I told her I'd be there on the dot, and she handed me the six parcels. Outside I stacked them carefully in the wire basket and set off. It had been easy coming into town. Now it was going to be all uphill and I was going to have to give it everything if I were to keep these fish suppers nice and hot. I wished I had a watch and could time myself, because whatever my record was for riding back from town I knew I was about to break it.

I arrived home, gasping and sweaty, to find Mum setting out the plates on the table, Christine spreading butter on the sliced bread, and Gillian taking a big pan of peas off the stove.

'Ah, here he comes,' Dad said, 'the man without whom ...'

'Mum, Dad, I've to go back and pay another twenty pence. They've got inflation and it's one pound twenty and we've got to take them money by tomorrow or – or – '.

'Or what?' Dad said.

'They didn't say.'

'But they let you go?' Mum said. 'Did they make you promise?'

'Aye, the woman at the till. And she had witnesses.'

Dad looked at his watch. 'Leave it to me,' he said. 'I'll drive down tonight, right after we've eaten. It's a credit to you, Michael, that they trusted you. Don't you think so, everybody?'

They did – and when we went back to the shop after tea, the woman in the chippy agreed.

'He looked a decent lad,' she said. 'Hungry too. So what else could I do?'

'What else indeed?' Dad said.

Gone Fishing

As I've already mentioned, Dad was a very clever man who continued to learn and grow in his mature years. I suppose these days you'd call him a bit of a late developer. He studied, at his own expense and in his own time, way into his thirties, and became highly qualified in his chosen field of electronic engineering. He acted and even looked like a boffin.

He was a man of few words, but they were always well chosen. Like many of the quieter types I've met in my life, he always thought before he answered a question – sometimes for such a long time that you'd think he hadn't heard you.

He liked peace and quiet, and was generally quite content with his own company. When he wasn't down the vegetable garden he was often in one of the outbuildings, or in his workshop, experimenting with things he was involved with at Vickers.

Other than spending time in the workshop or the garden, he liked to read. Mostly it was history, biography, technical stuff: he had piles of books, but not many novels. He hardly bothered with television, and indeed we were one of the last of all the families we knew to get one, when I was six or seven years old.

Dad must have found us kids a bit of a trial at times. We were a noisy bunch, always laughing, fighting, arguing and tearing around the place. 'Rambunctious', as Mum used to say.

Sometimes when we were in the living room with a gang of our mates from around the village, television blaring, and us all shouting at the tops of our voices, arguing over a game of Monopoly, the door would suddenly burst open and the handle would slam against the wall.

'Will you lot quieten down?' Dad would bellow at us. 'A fellow can't hear himself think in this house.'

It worked, by and large: he could be pretty intimidating when he blew his top, but while he could scare the living daylights out of any of our friends who hadn't got to know him, we knew it was all for effect. He was really a very kind and gentle man. He just liked good order. Sometimes, though, he really found it all too much and would send the visitors packing – and us to our bedrooms.

In other ways, though, Dad was quite go-ahead. We always had a car, for example, whereas even in the late 1960s and '70s, most families didn't.

In York nearly everybody went to work on their bikes. If ever you were in the city around knocking-off time you'd see hordes of them – a tidal wave, pouring out of Rowntrees or Terrys, or the railway carriage shops on Poppleton Road. The motorised traffic didn't stand a chance. Drivers just slammed their brakes on and waited for the wave to pass.

Being a bit further out of town, Dad decided it was a bit too far to cycle. Of course, we had the Morris Traveller, but I don't think it would have entered his head to drive in. Very few people did. No, the Traveller was for high days and holidays, and until we moved to Crayke it spent most of its long life in the garage.

The odd thing about Dad was that when he was a young man he'd actually owned a little Triumph. Many's the time we heard him wish he'd kept it.

'It'd be worth a packet today,' he'd say.

I remember trying to imagine my Dad dashing around the countryside in an open-top sports car. I gave it up – even though he once told me he'd gone up Whitwell Hill on the A64 at 100 miles an hour. It simply didn't fit. Once you've seen your Dad astride a mustard yellow KTM moped with a 49cc engine … well, you can see my point.

Ever more practical than stylish, Dad wore one of those old-fashioned peaked crash helmets with ear-flaps. Practical, yes. But cool? Not really. The machine itself was made in Austria. It had very little power, absolutely no style, but the important thing was it had amazing fuel economy.

Having said that, I suspect that Dad wasn't a natural on the moped. Mum was worried about it from the start, and rightly so. Once we'd moved out to Crayke she insisted he take the car in winter.

He'd had a number of minor accidents, mostly involving him losing balance and parting company with the machine. There was one that took place right outside my school. I was walking in with my mates when we heard a squeal of tyres and a bang. Turning round, I caught sight of Dad toppling off the bike. A car had tapped his rear end as it came out of a side-street. Dad was fine. He picked himself up and went on his way. He may have emerged unhurt from the incident, but I certainly didn't. I made the mistake telling everybody who he was, whereupon one of the boys started to make fun of me, telling me my Dad was a useless driver. Well, that did it. Before you could say 'knife' I had my jacket off and had him on the floor. The lollipop lady had to come and separate us.

I hope I'm not painting Dad as a bit of a wimp. Far from it. I think that deep down he wanted to have a more adventurous life. I'll never forget the time he took me and Phil to Bridlington for a fishing trip. I was wildly excited about it. I'd done river fishing of course, and I'd caught those codling off the rock at Hayburn Wyke, but I'd never been out to sea. I'd asked plenty of times but the answer had always been no, not yet; maybe when you're older.

It was a Sunday, and we were off in the car. Me, Phil and Dad. No girls, which made it feel all the more special. We had to be up at the crack of dawn for this one – well, six o'clock or thereabouts, but as it happened this was midsummer, so it barely got dark. Midsummer or not, however, Dad made sure we took thick sweaters and waterproof coats with us.

'You never know what to expect at sea,' he said. 'It can change in a minute.'

Because it was so early, Dad said it was all right to take the main road to the coast. He was right. There was hardly any traffic. Phil sat in the front next to him, and I was in the back, struggling to stay awake, despite the sun blazing in through the side window.

We pulled into Brid about eight o'clock and Dad treated us to a fried breakfast in one of the harbourside cafés. There was a bit of a breeze, and he said the best preventive for seasickness was a full stomach. We didn't need any persuading. We ordered bacon, egg, sausage, beans and toast and cleared our plates, wiping up the lovely bacon grease with an extra slice of bread the waitress brought us.

Our boat was what you'd call a proper boat. I doubt if it was twelve feet long. You could see the individual planks of which it was made, and it was painted a deep blue with white trim, and of course it had that crucial bit of red down near the waterline. All along the prow was a fat length of hempen rope, weathered and slightly frayed. A row of old tyres were hung over the side to stop it scraping against the harbour wall. A flag fluttered from the white painted mast, and, looking up at the captain's little cabin, we saw a shiny brass bell.

We paid our money and stepped aboard. There were eight or nine other customers, mostly men with grey hair and large stomachs. Two of them lugged a crate of beer aboard. They walked stiffly and slowly, and slumped gratefully onto the benches, catching their breath and lighting up their cigarettes. Even with just a dozen of us it was a bit of a squeeze. As we edged along the boat to find a perch on the wooden bench seats, we splashed through an inch or two of water that had gathered in the bottom. Dad must have seen the look on my face.

'Don't worry,' he said, 'it'll be rainwater. Either that or spray that's come over the side. Perfectly normal.'

We settled in our seats and listened as the skipper explained where we were going – and added that he couldn't guarantee a catch, but was hopeful. He looked at his watch, then at the sky, where a few clouds had gathered.

'Should be back in port by three,' he added. 'Everybody ready?'

'Aye aye, cap'n,' said the men with the crate – and promptly started opening the bottles. They handed one to Dad, but he shook his head.

'Just a bit early for me,' he laughed. 'Maybe later if the offer's still good.'

'You mean if we've any left,' the man said, putting the bottle to his lips and tipping his head back.

While all this was going on the captain had gone to his cabin, fired up the motor and was steering us out towards the open sea. We'd barely got outside of the harbour when the sun went in. The sea, which had been a lovely blue colour when we arrived, turned a leaden grey. The boat started to pitch more than was comfortable.

'Enjoying it, lads?' The old men seemed to think it was funny.

I gritted my teeth and assured them that I was. As it happened, it was quite good fun watching the bow rise and fall, and ducking the spray. Phil and I put up the hoods on our coats and hunched our shoulders against a stiff head-wind.

We hadn't gone very far when the captain came out and handed us our rods and lines. Then he brought us the bucket of bait, a seething mess of lugworm and cockles. We were just starting to bait the hooks when a fierce gust of wind rocked the boat, almost throwing me off balance. I dropped my rod and grabbed at the side. Dad put his hand to his forehead and scanned the sky.

'Hm, don't like the look of that,' he said. Away to the north a dark mass of cloud had gathered. 'See the rain?' he said.

We could. A milky-white sheet filled the sky between the base of the cloud and the horizon.

'Looks to be heading our way,' one of the old fellows said as he secured a wriggly worm onto his hook.

'Just the job, lad,' someone said. 'Bring them fish to t' surface.'

Just then the boat lurched as the wind gusted once more. Spray showered over us, soaking my knees.

'We going to be all right, Dad?' I said.

'Oh, don't worry,' he answered. 'Might be a bit uncomfortable, that's all.'

But ten minutes later, as the rain swept in and the waves piled higher and the water in the bottom of the little boat started to splosh this way and that with every lurch, he was looking decidedly worried – as was the captain.

'Sorry lads, but I'm going to turn her around,' he said.

There was general agreement that this wasn't a bad thing to do, a decision that was reinforced a moment later as a huge swell tossed us skyward, leaving my stomach somewhere in the bowels of the boat. That was followed by a truly sickening plunge into the following trough. As one of the old men heaved up his breakfast – and his beer – over the side, I started to feel decidedly queasy.

'We need to get rid of some of that water.' The captain was shouting through the open window. 'I need a couple of you to work the pumps.'

Dad didn't need any further invitation. He grabbed one pump handle, leaving me and Phil to work the other. As fast as we pumped the sea delivered fresh showers of salt water.

'We're not winning, but at least it's no worse,' Dad said, pausing for breath.

I carried on pumping. I was glad to have a job. It took my mind off my stomach, and the groans of other passengers. As we laboured our way towards the shore we heard the captain alerting the coastguard. Then he told his mate to get the distress flares out. That sent a shiver of fear through me, but Dad must have read my thoughts.

'Don't worry,' he said, 'it's a routine precaution.'

Looking back, I sometimes shudder when I recall that day. I suspect that we were in genuine danger for a while, despite what Dad said when we finally staggered ashore: 'All's well that ends well.'

Our captain was full of apologies. 'I did check the forecast,' he said, 'and it did speak of a squally shower, but later on. Not this early.'

He refunded us our money and offered us a free trip another time. Then Dad treated us to fish and chips on the harbour side, and a big mug of sweet tea. It put me off sea-fishing for a while, did that outing, but not our Phil. A few years later he joined the navy and eventually captained his own ship.

So we returned home empty-handed but happy enough, bursting to tell everyone about our adventure on the high seas. Dad, however, warned us about saying too much to Mum.

'Don't want her thinking we were in danger,' he said.

And it's those words, when I think of them, that persuade me that we probably were.

In the Bleak Midwinter

Mum said it was Dad's fault, the bitter weather that hit us that winter. She was only joking, of course, although at that age I couldn't be sure. It started when he came trudging back from the vegetable garden with a bunch of parsnips and an armful of leeks, his wellies all thick with mud.

'We just don't seem to get proper winters nowadays,' he said. 'I remember my Dad taking a pick-axe down the garden to lift a turnip for Mum's stew. Now you need waders. It's not natural, all this warm weather.' And then he said the fateful thing. 'What we need is a decent frost to kill off a few bugs. Put a bit of flavour in the parsnips too.'

'Be careful what you wish for,' Mum said, as she took the vegetables from him and dropped them in the old pot sink. 'And just be glad it's mild, with the heating system only half built.'

Of course, the weather changed. I don't think it had any choice.

Dad had been promising to take us to watch York City. They'd had a great run and got promoted to the old second division, playing teams like West Brom, Manchester United and Aston Villa. I think they were on the skids by this time, however, but Dad always said a true supporter would show up in good times or bad. Whatever the case, I was looking forward to the game, but as the week drew on the weather got colder and colder. The skies cleared, the wind dropped and we had three nights of frost – proper frost that clung to the trees and fell like a shower of desiccated coconut as soon as the slightest breeze blew.

'Never mind,' Dad said when he came home from work on the Friday. 'It seems to be clouding over, and there's a wind getting up. I dare say it'll rain in the night.'

It didn't rain. It snowed. Started as we sat down to our tea and was still coming down when I finally went to sleep about ten o'clock. Saturday morning we woke up to find it piled up on the window sills and banked up against the back door. And, as luck would have it, it was my turn to see to the morning chores.

I gave the fire a good poke, spread the usual double page of the previous night's Yorkshire Evening Press over the front of the grate and waited for it to draw. The back page news wasn't good. Racing at Wetherby was off. Rugby League was decimated. York City were 'doubtful' – and that was before the overnight blizzard. As I tried to read the caption, the page scorched, then burst into flames. I shoved it into the fire and watched it blaze away to nothing.

In the kitchen I prepared the feed for the hens and warmed up a big kettle of water. Then I stepped into my wellies and lugged the lot down the yard. The snow lay several inches deep, pure and white and powdery-soft. When I got to the gate I had to batter the frozen latch to loosen it. Inside, under the snow, the ground was a series of rock-hard ridges that all but tripped me up. The food steamed when I poured it into the trough. As expected, the drinking vessels were frozen solid. I dug out an old roasting tin from under the eaves of the shed, shook the snow out and tipped the contents of my kettle into it. Then I opened up. The hens trooped out, reluctantly, hesitantly, stepping daintily through the snow rather the way a bather would test the temperature of the North Sea on a summer's morning. They were followed by a subdued-looking cockerel. I went inside to look for eggs. Instead of the usual dozen or so I found four. Nothing like a spell of wintry weather to put the birds off their lay.

Back at the house everybody had gathered in the kitchen.

'Dad, Mum,' I said. 'Where's our sled?'

'The sled,' Dad said. 'Now there's a thing.'

I wasn't even sure whether we had a sled, or whether we'd borrowed one – it was so long since I'd been out on it. Two or three years, according to Dad.

'There just hasn't been enough snow,' he said. 'Last time I saw them they were in one of the outhouses. We'll have a look after breakfast, shall we?'

Dad had found uses for most of the outbuildings. One stored animal feed, another gardening equipment, a third was for bikes. The horses of course were stabled out there, but there was one that Mum called the outside glory-hole – to distinguish it from the cupboard under the stairs. That was where we threw deckchairs, spare balls, deflated space-hoppers, and all the other things that we couldn't find a place for when dusk was coming in and we were under orders to tidy the garden before bedtime. Maybe that was where the sled would be, she said.

We clambered over a mound of boxes, a rolled-up carpet and a spare car door before we found not one sled, but two, all dusty and speckled with droppings from the swallows that nested amongst the roof-spars every year. There was one sled that Dad had made when Christine was little, another that his dad had made for him when he was a lad. Same basic design, just a little older and slightly warped. We pulled them out and inspected them.

'Give them a bit of a brush down,' said Dad, 'and if we rub some candle grease on the runners they'll be fine. Otherwise they're good as new.'

We tidied them up as directed, wrapped ourselves up in our scarves and hats, and dragged them into the road, then up the hill towards the church. Half the neighbourhood was out there already, some on old sleds like ours, some on the new-fangled plastic jobs they'd picked up from one of the garages on the way to town, bright red and light as a feather. Others had sheets of old linoleum, bits of plywood with a string attached to the front, and some were on yellow plastic fertiliser sacks.

Between them they'd already turned Church Hill into a glistening sheet of ice. Someone had built a snowman too, and wrapped a York City scarf around him.

We stumbled to the top, with Petra dancing around our feet, and piled on board. Me and Phil on one sled, the girls plus the dog on the other. 'Race you!'

The girls were sitting upright, one behind the other. Phil had thrown himself flat on his face, and I lay on top of him. It was no contest. While they slithered down, dragging their feet like a couple of scaredy-cats, we gathered speed and shot past them like a bobsled on the Cresta Run. We were passing everybody on the slope.

It was only as we neared the bottom of the hill that I realised why Phil was suddenly shouting 'Brake brake brake!' at me. In front of us was a pile-up of sleds and bodies. The last thing I remember was the look on some lad's face as he realised we were heading straight for him. Not that Phil and I made contact. When the sled collided with the melee, we took off. I don't know how long we were airborne, but it seemed to last some time. In fact, looking back, I wish it had gone on a bit longer, because the landing was something I wouldn't want to re-live. Crunch went my face on the ice. I could taste the blood immediately.

A crowd gathered round. 'You all right?' someone asked.

I didn't answer. I put my hand to my nose and showed it to the on-lookers, all covered with blood.

Phil was okay. Typical of the luck he enjoyed back then, he'd landed on a girl – a rather fetching girl, as it happened: he later went out with her for a few weeks. Anyway, once he'd introduced himself to her, he saw what had happened to me and fetched Dad, who reluctantly got the car out and took me into the now-familiar YDH – York District Hospital. In casualty they told me I'd broken my nose.

On the bright side, I arrived home with an authentic black eye, and couldn't wait to show it off at school on the Monday. Once we got home, however, the question uppermost in my mind was: when could I go sledding again?

The answer was: not till it snows again – because that night the temperature rose, the rain Dad had predicted arrived, and all that remained in the morning was a smudge of white and a sodden red-and-blue scarf where the snowman had been, plus a couple of streaks of rapidly melting ice on Church Hill. Next day the sleds went back in the glory-hole and stayed there for another year.

That was far from my last visit to casualty. Later that year I went fishing out at Nunnington, on the River Rye. Using a hand-line to try and catch a trout I'd spotted, I let it slip, allowing the hook to embed itself in my middle finger. It dug deep, right to the bone. I had all on not to burst into tears, but brightened at the prospect of another visit with my favourite nurses.

Just when the staff at YDH thought they'd seen the last of the Pannetts, it was Christine's turn to show up. That too was my doing. I challenged her to a bike race down Church Hill, got in her way – and over she went, knocking out one of her front teeth. As Phil said, girls were nothing but trouble … so the fact that I consented to spend a week with a whole gang of them the following summer probably needs a little explaining.

Girl Guide For a Week

'Now Michael, have you packed enough underwear?'

'Yes, Mum.'

'Quite sure?'

'Yes, Mum.'

'Socks?'

'Yes, Mum.'

'Clean shirt for Sunday?'

'Look, Mum, I packed everything you set out for me.'

'Good. Because I don't want you running around looking like a tramp. And I'm certainly not doing any washing while we're away. I've enough on my plate as it is without worrying about the state of your underwear.'

There was always tension in the air when Mum went on one of her camping trips with the Girl Guides. First she'd fuss around making sure there was plenty of food in the freezer – and a roster of daily menus on the wall above the kitchen table. Then she'd write lists of things that had to be done while she was away. There would be notes about putting the dustbin out on Tuesday, paying the milkman on Friday, the newsagent on Saturday – and the money would all be counted out in separate, labelled brown envelopes. There would be reminders about the washing, about feeding the animals, about changing the sheets at the end of the week. And, in the days running up to her departure she'd go over it all several times, just to make quite sure we'd got it.

It was the same every year, and it soon came to the point where we were hardly listening, just nodding agreement to everything she said: anything to get her out of the door. The difference this time was that I was going with her – very much against my will.

I complained. I whined. I argued. But she wasn't having it.

'I'm not leaving you here unsupervised,' she said. 'I know you. You'll either end up setting fire to the place or breaking something. Most likely one of your bones. I don't want to come home and find you in York District Hospital with your arm in plaster.'

'But what about Phil?' I pleaded. 'You're letting him stay at home. Why can't I?'

'He's older than you. And far more responsible.'

'But I'm older too. I'm going to be in year six in September. Senior school next.'

'Yes, and when you get there you'll find out that you've an awful lot of growing up to do.'

'Well, if Phil's responsible doesn't that mean he can be in charge of me? I mean, he's almost fifteen. You know I'll do what he says.'

I was going to add that he'd give me a thick ear if I didn't, but thought better of it. In any case, Phil was there in the room while this particular conversation took place. He didn't say a word. He was keeping his head down. He was desperate to have me out of the way so that he could spend more time with his girlfriend. The girlfriend that nobody knew about. Except me, that is – but he'd threatened me with destruction if I dared breathe a word about her.

'But Mum, I'll be good. I promise I will. I'll be really, really good. Honestly.'

'Yes, I'm sure you will,' she said. 'Because you'll be under my supervision – where I can keep an eye on you. We've been over this till I'm sick of it. You're coming with me and the girls, and that's final.'

And so I went. And hated it. Being surrounded by a bunch of girls all week, and being expected to take part in their activities, was not my idea of a good time at all. I can admit it now: I did more than my fair share of sulking. And I vowed it would be different next time.

It certainly was. The following year I prepared myself. I had a plan. I told Mum I would agree to come, and would promise not to be a whingeing pest. All she had to do was allow me to bring my mate Mark. Mum liked that. It made sense. Not only was Mark's mother a fellow Guide leader – and a good friend – but Mum had always thought of Mark as a nice lad. She thought he was a good influence on me. I got into less trouble with him than with my other mates. Well, of course I did. Mark was a very slippery customer, a master of cunning excuses.

Her view might have been different if she'd connected him with the mysterious youth in a balaclava helmet who tied a bunch of bangers to a piece of wood that time and set it off, torpedo-fashion, across the pond in Rowntree Park. But everybody knew that was some fifteen year old, a local youth. They knew it because Mark spread the rumour – once he'd emerged, weak with laughter, from his hiding-place around the corner by the tennis courts.

And it was a good job she never made a connection between Mark and that young tearaway disguised in a Batman mask who strapped a pair of sky-rockets under his saddle one November evening and pedalled down our road trailing a shower of multi-coloured flames behind his bike. But why should she? As far as she was aware it was as we told her: some young hooligan from the next village; and when she reflected that such behaviour would lead a boy to approved school we nodded in agreement with her, and even tried to tut-tut the way she did.

Sometimes when I look back to those days I go hot and cold all over, thinking of what we got away with. And the outrageous lies we told. But the fact is we were very good at deception. Mum totally fell for the idea that Mark was a nice, well-behaved lad, and a good example to others. She once went so far as to say, in Mark's presence, that he was a sensible fellow and would do well in life.

And she was right. He did do well – but not in the way she expected. His surname was Addy and he went on to become an actor, making his name as one of the male strippers in The Full Monty. But back then he was no more than an ordinary Yorkshire lad, co-opted with me into the Guides and ready to brave a week under canvas down by the River Derwent.

We had quite a time of it. Whereas the previous year I'd moped around, trying to wriggle out of all the fun that had been organised for the girls, this year it finally dawned on me that there was much to be gained by getting stuck in and showing the lasses what I was capable of.

So there I was, climbing trees, jumping from the highest branches and splashing into the river; or turning over the kayaks and re-surfacing with a grin on my face; wrestling with Mark before a shrieking audience of twelve- and thirteen-year-old girls; daring each other to race barefoot across the dying embers of the camp-fire.

This was a pivotal time in my life; it was the moment when I realised there was nothing I wouldn't do if it won me an admiring smile from a good-looking girl. As for the injuries, the cuts and bruises and blisters, they were badges of honour, a minor inconvenience to be suffered in the cause of attracting the admiration of the fair sex. The bloodier the injuries, the more solicitous they were. The greater the pain the more likely that we'd get to experience the sweet delight of being given first aid at the hands of a bonny little troop leader. We may have been on our school holidays but we were getting an education. Not only that, but at night there was homework.

'Mark! Mike!' We'd had supper round the camp fire; we'd had our cocoa; we'd sung the National Anthem, had roll-call and been sent to our tents.

'Mark! Mike!' It was a loud stage whisper and it seemed to echo round our corner of the campsite.

'Mike! Mark!'

Mark was already sitting up. I switched on my torch. We looked at each other.

'Is that you they're calling?' I said.

'I thought it was you.'

'Mike! Mark!'

Mark nudged me. 'Nah, it's both of us.'

We were out of our sleeping bags and at the opening of the little tent, poking our heads out into the cool night air. From the tent Mum shared with Mark's mother, over in the corner of the field, came the murmur of their portable television, wired up to the car battery.

'What is it?' I whispered, as loud as I dare.

'We're having a party.'

We didn't answer. We didn't know what to say. After a long silence, followed by a lot of girlish tittering, came the magic words:

'Well, are you lads coming or what? We want to play Midnight Beast.'

The boldness of the invitation threw us at first. We'd been brought up to think of girls as shy, retiring creatures; we believed that it was our role to pursue them, and that their role was to run away from us, shrieking. The idea that they would wantonly invite us into their tent after dark – well, it left us somewhere between shock and wonder.

We threw our clothes on, crept outside and made our way to the tent from which the invitation seemed to have come. As we approached it we could see flickers of torchlight illuminating the bulging canvas. When the opening was unzipped we crawled inside. It was a tight squeeze. There must have been a dozen Guides in a tent designed to accommodate six – but we weren't complaining.

It was all very innocent, but it wasn't half fun. We played cards, scoffed crisps and sweets, and drank pop. We told jokes and boasted about all sorts of wicked things we'd never done, and we shivered with the excitement of knowing that we were supposed to be in bed in our own tents – even as we reminded each other to keep our voices down in case the grown-ups heard us.

In that delicious hour or two I fell in love – as I was prone to do many times over the next few years. Her name was Helen, she was a year or two older than me, and she was beautiful.

Some time after midnight Mark and I sneaked back to where we were supposed to be, and stayed awake for another hour, evaluating the charms of the various girls and each laying claim to a particular favourite and challenging each other to see who could kiss the most girls over the rest of the week.

Mark won, but I only had his count to go on. I knew he was exaggerating, so I did a bit of my own 'massaging the figures' to try and impress him. I was to learn later on in life that, where girls are concerned, all blokes exaggerate. Anyway, I never worked out what Mark had that I didn't, but the girls seemed to find him irresistible. As the week went on I slowly realised that I was in the presence of a master.

That was our first and, sadly, our last holiday with the girls. By the time the next year's trip came around, both my Mum and Mark's had overheard enough little bits of gossip from their charges to work out what was going on. Happy days – but they were soon over.

And no sooner had we returned home than it was time to go shopping for our new school uniforms. Senior school beckoned, and another phase of my childhood was about to begin ...

Acknowledgements

Special thank you to Alan Wilkinson,
and all at Country Publications and the Dalesman team.

A little bit extra

Readers from all over the world – and people I meet when I do my talks and other events – often ask me about Yorkshire and its people so here are some helpful websites:

Welcome to Yorkshire *yorkshire.com*
Visit York *visityork.org*
Yorkshire Tea (brilliant brew & support) *yorkshiretea.co.uk*
Grand Central Railways (great transport & support) *grandcentralrail.com*
Black Sheep Brewery (great beer & support) *blacksheepbrewery.com*

And finally …

If you want to help a deserving cause – and people you might need one day – the local mountain and cave rescue teams all do a great job. They're volunteers who go out in all weathers and the service depends on donations:

Scarborough and Ryedale Mountain Rescue Team *srmrt.org.uk*
Swaledale Mountain Rescue Team *swaledalemrt.org.uk*
Cleveland Search and Rescue Team *csrt.co.uk*
Cave Rescue Organisation *cro.org.uk*
Upper Wharfedale Fell Rescue Association *uwfra.org.uk*